Tracks ALONG the TRAIL of LIFE

A COLLECTION OF SHORT STORIES

LIFE OF A VETERINARIAN, RANCHER, PILOT & PASTOR

BILL HINES

Tracks
Along the Trail of Life

© 2021, Bill Hines.

Print ISBN: 978-1-09837-4-020

eBook ISBN: 978-1-09837-4-037

As we walk along the trail of life, we follow the tracks of those who have gone before. If we live long enough, we may find that we have come full circle and the tracks we are now following are our own.

BILL HINES
2021

KITTY AND
THE JACKPOT DAY

I t was deep into the fall of the first year after I bought the veterinary clinic, and I had been running hard for several months.

Getting in after dark one Saturday evening after a long day of pregnancy testing, I was entertaining thoughts of a hot shower, something to eat and a long rest, when the clinic phone rang.

A panic filled woman's voice said, "My little boy's kitten got run through the clothes dryer, can I bring him in?"

They soon arrived at the clinic, in much less time than it should have taken, and the story came out.

She was a teacher at one of the reservation schools to the north. She had a son, Tommy, who was between two and three years old. He was small for his age, and his speech was slow developing. In fact, the only two words he had mastered so far were Mommy and Kitty.

Kitty was his much beloved cat and was about four or five months old.

The woman was a single mother, and she sure didn't need this added stress to an already stressful life.

She had been doing weekend laundry, was emptying the dryer, got distracted and went off with the dryer door open. When she came back, she closed the door and started the dryer again.

Meanwhile, Kitty, with a cat's unerring knack for finding warm places, hopped into the dryer, and settled down for a nap.

After a while, the lady heard Tommy giggling and saying, "Kitty."

She continued with her work, but later she heard Tommy saying, "Mommy, Kitty."

Going to investigate, she found Tommy pointing to the dryer and saying, "Kitty."

Sure enough, there was Kitty, going around and around in the dryer. She quickly retrieved him and called the clinic.

The lady placed the most dehydrated little scrap of a kitten I had ever seen on the exam table. Things didn't look good. We would need all the help we could get to pull this one through.

I listened to the heart, and it was still working, though obviously struggling. Occasionally Kitty would take a shallow breath.

The eyes were sunk back so far, I could hardly see them, and when I pinched up a little tent of skin, it stayed right there instead of pulling back into position as it should.

Knowing there was no chance of finding a vein on the leg with this much dehydration, I clipped the hair off the neck and tried to find the vein in the neck. No luck, so, I surgically scrubbed the neck and taking a scalpel blade, carefully cut down through the skin to reveal the jugular vein.

Though the blood was moving very slowly, I finally got enough to pool in the jugular vein that I could get my smallest IV catheter into the vein. I stitched the hub of the catheter to the skin as I closed it up, then wrapped it in place with some pink Vet Wrap. Then came hooking a bag of fluid to an IV hose and connecting it to the catheter.

By now, the lady's eyes were wide, and she said, "Doctor, how much might this cost? I don't have hardly any money."

I glanced at Tommy, looking up over the side of the exam table, his eyes fixed on Kitty. I glanced also at the lady, but what I was seeing was a vision of myself and my own mother, as she sat at the table, her head in her hands, trying desperately to find a way to keep body and soul together for her children, after my father left.

In my gruffest voice, I said, "Mam, the first thing we have to do is save Kitty's life. There will be no more talk of paying until we accomplish that."

I knew I was just kicking the can down the road, and we would have to deal with it at some point, but I needed time to think.

I glanced again at Tommy. By now, his lower lip was trembling, and tears filled his eyes. It was time to treat the client as well as the patient.

Looking at Tommy, I said, "Mam, could you lift Tommy up so he can help hold the bag of fluid? I need a steady hand to help."

She caught my drift, and lifted Tommy up. I handed Tommy the bag and said, "Now Tommy, I need for you to hold this tight, right at this level, OK?"

Tommy's lip stopped trembling and set in a firm line. He was on a mission to save Kitty.

I left them standing that way while I took Furacin ointment, gauze pads and Vet Wrap and bandaged up Kitty's burnt foot pads.

He looked somewhat festive, in spite of his condition, with a pink neck wrap and pink stockings.

There was a new steroid that the salesmen facetiously called "Life in a Bottle", that was supposed to be just the thing for battling shock.

Well, Kitty would certainly be in shock, so I administered some of this new medicine, called Solu-Delta-Cortef.

Finally, I got an IV stand, took the bag of fluid from Tommy, and hung it on the stand. "That's all we can do for now," I said, "I'll check back on him later tonight."

The lady went out, carrying Tommy, who was reaching over her shoulder and plaintively saying over and over, "Kitty, Kitty."

At midnight, there was no change, but about a fourth of the fluid was gone. I increased the drip slightly and went home.

At four a.m. there was still no change, but more fluid was gone. I turned Kitty to his other side. Pneumonia was sure to become an issue if he survived at all. I switched to a new bag of fluid and went home.

Sunday morning, I thought his eyes looked a little better. Put one small check mark in the "hopeful" column.

After church, more of the fluid was gone, and I found that the towel I had put under Kitty was slightly wet. Put another small mark in the "hopeful" column. Now that I knew his kidneys were working, we could begin to treat for pneumonia.

That evening when I went in, I heard a faint "Meow", and also found that the fresh towel under Kitty was soaked. Put a little bigger check mark in the "hopeful" column.

Next morning, Kitty was sitting up, and the fresh towel was again soaked. I got some beef broth from the refrigerator, warmed it up until it was just tepid on the back of my hand, filled a small syringe with it and put this in Kitty's mouth.

I was rewarded by a little pink tongue trying to lap the broth. Kitty took a couple of syringes full of broth, then laid back down.

Kitty got more medicine for pneumonia, and I switched to a new bag of fluid.

By the next evening, Kitty would eat a small amount of canned cat food as well as lap the broth.

We continued to treat for pneumonia, and Kitty improved rapidly, so that by Friday evening, he was ready to go home.

When the young mother and Tommy came to pick him up that evening, she was adamant, "Doctor, I must know what this will cost, I'm afraid I'll have to make payments."

By now, I'd had time to think up a plan.

"Mam," I said, "I have a policy here that every tenth cat that comes in, I treat for free. I call it Jackpot Day, as in hitting the jackpot. And Kitty came in on Jackpot Day."

There wasn't a scrap of truth to the tale, but as the missionary lady in the movie, Rooster Cogburn said, after she told the judge a whopper, "If thine intent be pure."

I hoped the Lord would forgive my deception.

I saw Kitty every few months, as I put him on a strict vaccination and deworming regimen, and you know, that Kitty was the luckiest little feline I ever saw; he hit the Jackpot Day every visit.

You've heard of a win-win situation?

Well, there are times that life gives us the opportunity for a win-win-win situation, and Kitty and the Jackpot Day was one of those times.

Kitty purred contentedly on Tommy's shoulder, as Tommy grinned for all he was worth. The young mother wouldn't have to choose between paying a vet bill, and more urgent needs, and I could sleep peacefully without thoughts of my own mother's struggles burning in my belly.

Yep, Kitty and the Jackpot Day was a win-win-win situation.

EMILY AND POGO

Emily was in her early 80's when I first met her. She lived in a trailer house on a small acreage a few miles from town, with a milk cow, a few beef cows, a few pigs and a dog named Pogo.

Pogo was a small, spotted dog, mongreled and many fathered, but she was a kind-hearted little creature, who had the endearing habit of running to meet me when she saw my pickup coming.

She would run ahead of me back to the house, whirling in circles and every so often leaping straight up like a person on a pogo stick, thus her name.

The first time Emily called me out, I wondered about all the grass and weeds growing in the tracks of her two-track lane. Apparently, Emily didn't leave the place often and didn't have many visitors.

Emily had been a teacher at one of the reservation schools near where she lived, and she was a wealth of knowledge about what the reservation was like in the "old days."

Emily had been widowed for many years, but as she said, it didn't make much difference; her husband never worked, and as she termed it, spent most of his time, "tom catting around."

She was the one who told me the origin of the name Bear in The Lodges Creek, which runs through our ranch, though we didn't own it at that time. And the name was pretty descriptive!

My first call to Emily's place was for her milk cow, which was down and unable get up.

When I pulled up to her place, she met me in the yard. She was wearing striped overalls and had a bandana tied on her head to keep her hair arranged though stray wisps of gray were escaping on both sides.

The lines and fissures of her weather-beaten face crinkled into a smile as she shook my hand and said, "Hello Doc, I'm Emily."

She led the way to a run-down old barn that had once been red long ago, but the relentless South Dakota sun plus the wind driven snows of many winters had weathered the barn to gray.

The barn listed slightly to one side, beginning to give it a kinship to the famous Leaning Tower of Pizza.

There was a loft in the barn which Emily's nephews filled with hay for her each summer and a ladder led to the loft.

Emily climbed this ladder each day to pitch down hay for the milk cow, and any calves living in the barn.

The cow had calved a few days earlier and was now in sternal recumbency with her head around to the side.

Her temperature was sub-normal, and her position and history confirmed hypocalcemia, or as it is commonly known, "milk fever."

The treatment for milk fever is to run calcium-phosphorus solution IV, but it has to be done carefully, as it can stop the heart and cause an almost dead cow to become a fully dead cow.

I got a halter from the pickup, and tied the cows head to her hind leg, as cows often respond fairly quickly, and I didn't want her jumping up before I was finished.

Emily wanted to know why I was tying the cow's head, and I said, "She might want to get up before I'm finished."

Emily looked at me dubiously, the wrinkles on her face creased into a smile of unbelief, but said nothing.

I got an IV set up, had Emily hold the bottle while I got a needle into the cow's jugular vein, then, very slowly, while listening to the heart with my stethoscope, I ran the bottle in.

By the time all the calcium-phosphorus solution was in the cow, she was straining to get her head loose, and I had barely finished gathering my things up, when the cow rose slowly and shakily to her feet.

"Well, I'll be," said Emily in surprise, "let's go in and have some coffee."

In the house, Emily boiled coffee in a gallon tin can, then strained it through a dish towel into a pan, saying, "My mother-in-law always told me, 'grounds in the coffee are grounds for divorce.'"

Over the years, Emily had me in for coffee many times, and she always made it the same way, and always repeated that phrase.

For a while, nothing went wrong at Emily's place, so I only saw her when she had me out to vaccinate piglets or calves.

A few years later, Emily came into the vet clinic carrying Pogo in a basket. Emily was obviously distraught.

"I think she's been poisoned," Emily said, "she's having seizures and can hardly breathe."

I set the dog on the table, noticing how rigid her muscles were and how difficult it was for her to get her breath.

Pogo had given birth to several pups a few days before, and although the symptoms were different for her than they had been for the milk cow, it was hypocalcemia, called "Eclampsia" in dogs.

I very carefully and slowly ran some calcium-phosphorus solution into her vein, while monitoring her heart.

Within a few minutes, the rigid muscles began to relax, her heart settled down, and she was soon back to normal.

Emily is the only client I ever had who experienced hypocalcemia in both a cow and a dog.

After that episode, Emily had me spay Pogo. She didn't want a repeat of the terrifying eclampsia event.

The years sped by, and I saw Emily once in a while as I treated a sick animal, or vaccinated pigs or calves for her.

One day Emily came into the clinic leading Pogo on a leash. Both were now quite old and arthritic, in fact Emily's hands were now gnarled and twisted even more than when I first met her.

I set Pogo on the exam table while Emily explained the reason for her visit to the vet today.

There was a mass on Pogo's belly that Emily was concerned about. As I examined the lump, I got a sinking feeling in my stomach.

It was melanoma, a very aggressive form of cancer and x-rays revealed that it had metastasized to the lungs.

I explained the situation to her, and Emily and I both knew that this was the end of the line for Pogo.

"Emily, do you want some time alone with Pogo before we proceed," I asked. "No," she replied, let's just get on with what has to be done."

Emily stroked Pogo's head as I slipped a needle into the vein on the leg and administered the euthanasia solution. Pogo just gently faded into sleep, never to wake again.

Emily said, "Would you carry her to the pickup for me, Doc?"

I carried Pogo out, and laid her in the seat, with her head on Emily's lap.

"Get in," Emily ordered.

I got in on the passenger seat and held Emily's hand while she cried softly. After some time, she wiped her eyes and said, "I'm alright now Doc, get out."

I stepped out of the pickup, and watched an era end, as Emily drove away.

DOBIE

THE DOBERMAN

It was late spring of my first year in practice after buying the vet clinic. Schools were out by then, and my four daughters were hanging out in the clinic one morning when a fellow came in with a big Doberman dog.

He was a teacher at one of the reservation schools, but was moving to Florida to start a new job.

He couldn't take the dog with him, for whatever reason, and hadn't been able to give it away, so brought it in to be put to sleep.

Meantime, in the waiting room, my girls were all over the dog, petting him and he was eating up all this attention.

When it came the teacher's turn, he led the Doberman into the exam room and told me the situation, and that he needed the dog put to sleep.

The girls had come into the room through another door and heard what was about to happen. They set up a howl of protest.

"No Daddy, don't kill Dobie, he's nice Daddy, Dobie won't bite anyone, please Daddy, we could take him."

By now, tears were falling, but I could envision this creature who was as big as a small horse eating a half a sack of dog food per day. And they already had one dog, we really didn't need another one, but.........

Four precious little faces looked up at me with big sad eyes. The teacher looked at me with big sad eyes, the Doberman looked at me with big sad eyes.

What could I do? I was out gunned. There was nothing to do but surrender with whatever dignity I could muster, so I said, "OK, you can keep him."

The girls were ecstatic, the teacher was happy, the dog was lapping up all the happiness. I was skeptical.

But the girls were right, Dobie never did bite anyone, but he would sure make you think he was going to.

He turned out to be a great protector and companion for the girls, and he hardly barked at most people, but at some point, in his past, he must have been abused by a person who was drunk, because he hated anyone who had been drinking, and could seem to sense that they had been.

One evening, just at dusk, as I was closing up the clinic, a car pulled up near the back door, and a man got out who was staggering drunk.

He tottered toward the door, holding on to his car to stay upright. He had just reached about even with the front tire on his car when Dobie came roaring out from under the truck unloading chute barking like he was going to tear the man apart.

The guy froze in position. You could almost see his addled brain trying to decide if he should make a run for the door, or retreat to his car door.

Dobie kept him frozen in position, baying at him in a manner that must have been terrifying for the poor fellow.

Now, as I said earlier, the kids had another dog, a little Pomeranian that was a ball of fur and pure evil.

You've no doubt heard the story of when Jesus cast a bunch of demons out of the man at Gadera? The demons went into a herd of pigs, who then ran down the hill into the sea and drowned.

Have you ever wondered if the demons drowned with the pigs?

I have it on good authority that they did not.

Somehow, they found their way to America, and all took up residence in this Pomeranian named Sparky.

So, as Dobie held the guy transfixed, Sparky shot out from under his car and bit him on the heel.

An amazing transformation occurred. One minute the man could hardly walk, the next minute, he could fly.

He rose up as if by levitation and landed on his back on the hood of his car, then went crawling like a crawdad up the windshield onto the roof, with Dobie baying in his face and acting like he was going to eat the guy.

It took me a couple of minutes to stop laughing enough to go out, call Dobie off and send Sparky scampering to the house with his tail between his legs.

Dobie furnished quite a bit of entertainment over the years that he was with us, although never as much as that evening when he performed the miracle of making the man fly.

He was so big that the smaller girls could ride him, and he didn't consume half a sack of dog food per day, although sometimes I thought he got close.

SADDLE BRONCS,
YAKS AND A FOOT ROT COW

One of my first calls after buying the vet clinic was from a fellow near Pine Ridge, named Bud.

He ranched on the reservation, though he was not Indian. He owned some private land and leased a lot of other land.

It was shortly before sundown when he called and said, "I've got a cow with foot rot, can you come out and treat her?" I said, "Yes, get her in and I'll be right out."

"Oh, she can't walk," he replied, "we'll have to treat her where she is."

I got there just after sundown, only to discover that the cow could not only walk, she could also run, at a pretty good clip, even with her swollen and sore foot.

There was a spare tire mounted on the front of my pickup, and Bud said, "I'll sit on your spare tire, you put me up on her and I'll rope her."

Now, neither of us gave any consideration to what we would do once he did get a rope on her, since there was nothing to dally up to, but he mounted the spare, and we were off.

Bud was swinging his rope, and we were gaining on the cow, when she suddenly disappeared down a washout.

I stomped on the brakes and turned hard to the left to keep from going in after her.

Bud shot off the spare tire as if from a catapult, rolled over and over, then lay groaning.

I parked the pickup and rushed down into the washout, helped him up and got him back into the cab of my pickup.

We spent the rest of the evening taking him to the hospital in Gordon, Nebraska for x-rays and treatment of a broken collar bone.

When I finally got him home, he didn't give me the cursing I probably deserved, and even insisted on filling my pickup with gas for all the extra running around.

The cow got well on her own.

I've seen this happen several times, that a foot rot cow couldn't be caught, but chasing her to try, increased the circulation in the lame foot, and healing occurred anyway.

Sometime later, Bud pulled into the clinic with a long trailer filled with saddle broncs and yaks. He wanted to take them to a rodeo in Canada, and we needed to do some blood tests before I could fill out the international health certificate.

The horses had been handled enough due to being hauled to rodeos all over that they were fairly easy to get blood from, and we put them in a pen at the end of the alley behind the clinic.

The yaks were a different matter.

They had never been handled and wanted no part of our program nor of going to Canada.

The only way to get blood was to catch them one at a time in the head gate inside the clinic, draw blood from the tail vein, put an ID tag in their ear, then release the head gate and let them back out.

The first one worked fine, and when I released the head gate, it backed out, ran down the alley and turned into the open pen across from the broncs.

When the second one came out of the head gate, instead of turning in to the pen with the first one, it jumped over the end of the alley and headed for town.

The first thing it would come to in town was the grade school.

Bud grabbed a couple of bridles from the overhead of his trailer and yelled, "Come on. I think a couple of those broncs are broke to ride."

Recalling the foot rot cow, I was more than a little skeptical about this program, but the thought of that yak running amuck on a playground full of children overcame my trepidation, and I grabbed a handful of the horse's mane and swung on.

To my immense relief, the broncs were indeed broke to ride, and by a combination of chase and be chased, we got the yak back to the clinic and into the pen with the first one.

Everything went fine then until the last one, which was the biggest and rowdiest.

It had wide horns, but somehow, I managed to get the headgate closed on it.

Once I got it bled and released the headgate, instead of backing up as the others had, it jumped forward, slamming the headgate open, and was loose in the large animal room.

At the time, my sister was running a little dog grooming business out of the clinic and had groomed a little FeFe poodle that morning and put it in a cage on the floor of the large animal room to await its owner.

Seeing the yak making laps around the room, the poodle began to bark. This annoyed the yak, and it started butting the cage all around the room, with the poodle yelping in terror.

I finally got the back door open, waved something in the yak's face to get it to chase me, and ran out the door, with the yak hot on my heels.

Bud and I got the yaks and broncs loaded, and he pulled away. I was never so glad to see a trailer leave the clinic.

A few days later, I saw the lady who owned the poodle at the post office. She said, "Your sister must have mistreated FeFe, he was scared to death when I picked him up."

Since she was quite elderly and high strung, I was afraid to tell her what actually happened, as she might have a heart attack, so, I said nothing.

Sometimes it's best to let sleeping dogs lie.

GELDING WILD STALLIONS

In the mid 70's the Bureau of Land Management was trying to thin down the numbers of wild horses on the public lands in Wyoming, Utah and Nevada.

They came up with a scheme to have private citizens "adopt" the horses and take them away, thus relieving the BLM of the responsibility of taking care of all the ones that had been captured.

With typical bureaucratic bungling, there were lots of rules and regulations, and no one had thought through what they were trying to do.

So, the public would adopt the young horses and mares, but refused to have anything to do with the stallions, as they were nearly impossible to handle without really good facilities, which of course the average citizen didn't have.

This left the BLM with lots of older stallions that no one wanted. Although horse slaughter was still legal at that time, the BLM made the rule that the horses had to be held a certain amount of time before this could happen.

They put out the call for anyone to take large groups of these old stallions, basically for free, if the citizen would keep them for two years.

Several of my rodeo stock contractor clients thought that these might make good bucking horses and "adopted" truck loads to use for broncs.

One client got seventy head of them that ranged in age from about six years old to truly ancient.

Now males of nearly all species, including our own are prone to fighting if crowded together too much, and these old studs were no exception. So, this client called me out to geld these stallions, since they were fighting so much, they were tearing up his facilities.

He had a large corral, with a long alley that led to a heavily built bucking chute.

Many of the older horses had long "broom" tails and the stock contractor wanted these shortened up so they weren't dragging in the mud and getting full of cockle burrs.

To do this, he had a broad axe, and had a man put a block of wood under the tail and chop off the excess with the axe.

The crew that day consisted of mostly young guys who had just been bailed out of the detox facility for a day of work.

Most of these knew little about horses and were not interested in learning anytime soon.

There were also a couple of cowboys who were mounted, and in the big corral with the studs. They were armed with whips, to protect them from the studs. They would sort one off and run him down the alley into the bronc chute, where the boss would slide the tail gate shut.

Usually, the stud proceeded to try to kick the tail gate to pieces. Fortunately, it was heavy built, so it held up.

To round out the crew, there was a red haired "pilgrim" from Missouri who was hitch hiking through the country, who had no intention of touching a horse, and who talked incessantly about the virtues of his water pipe. He only lasted until after lunch, which was his only reason for being there to start with, to get a free lunch.

So, with a horse in the bronc chute, we would throw a soft rope over his neck, then reach under his neck with a stiff wire and draw the end to us. One dared not reach into the chute, as the horse would bite anyone who did.

We would pass one end of the rope over a board about neck high, and the other end under the same board.

By twisting the ends, this drew the horse's neck over close enough that I could get a needle in his vein without getting bitten.

I would give him 1 ½ to 2 cc of succinylcholine, pull off the rope and swing the gate open.

The stud would take three or four jumps into the arena and go end over end, whereupon, one man would jump on his head, another would pull the uphill leg forward to give me access, and the axe man, who was a huge individual, would put a block of wood under the tail and whack with the broad axe.

The problem we faced was that succinylcholine only held the horse down for about a minute to a minute and a half.

So, for me, it was slice, pull, crunch, slice, pull, crunch, drop my instruments into a bucket of disinfectant and race for the nearest fence.

The old studs were more than a little offended at us taking such indiscrete liberties and would come to have a word with anyone still in the arena when they got to their feet.

The axe man was more concerned with escaping to the fence than he was with where his axe landed, so some tails got cut long, and some were so short they were nearly to the bone.

Between the flying axe, the striking hooves, and the snapping teeth, I had to step lively all day to preserve my own anatomy intact.

It was a long day, and we were all glad when the job was finished. Unfortunately, only two of the horses ever made good broncs, and the rest would just run off, crash into fences, or try to jump them, and hurt themselves and/or their riders.

I don't have any knowledge of what happened to the rest of them.

There were some horses "adopted" by other stock contractors that turned out to be good broncs, but I don't think there were many.

COLD WEATHER CALVING

The first year I was at Martin; after finishing the big run of fall work; pregnancy testing cows and preconditioning calves, things settled down to Bangs vaccinating heifers from early January on, plus small animal work and some horse work.

On Feb. 15 I got my first night call for a heifer that couldn't have her calf. A number of the local ranchers had bred their heifers to Longhorn bulls the summer before.

Longhorn calves were usually smaller than Hereford or Angus, so they reasoned that their heifers should calve easier.

Unfortunately, a lot of the bulls they bought were only Longhorn cross-breds, so some of the calves were too big to be born naturally.

So, the heifers started coming into the clinic for C-Sections at an ever-increasing pace. In fact, by the first of March there was one day that I did eleven C-Sections in a single twenty-four hour period.

Several of the ranchers enjoyed coming to town to visit with their neighbors and have a few drinks, even during calving season; so, I frequently got a call from them about midnight on up to shortly after two a.m., when the bars closed.

It never seemed to occur to them that not everyone was awake at that time of night.

By April, I had gone without sleep enough that I was so crabby I could hardly stand myself, but that didn't slow them down any.

Occasionally, some rancher couldn't get his heifer to the clinic for whatever reason.

One afternoon I got a call from up on the reservation to go do a C-Section on a heifer that the rancher was unable to get to a corral for loading. When he tried to move her, she would strain, then go down.

It was a cold day, spitting snow and with a vicious north wind. When I got there, I found that the heifer was out on a hilltop, near the highway.

I drove around the hill and through the pasture to where she was. We got a halter on her, got her to her feet and tied her head to the grill guard of my pickup.

She could still move around far too much for me to do surgery, so I looped a lariat around her neck then ran it along her left side, around behind the cab of the pickup and tied it to the grill guard on the other side.

This made a fairly effective emergency pasture squeeze chute.

There was no electricity anywhere near, so I couldn't clip the hair off her side as I usually did.

Instead, I scrubbed her left side, then taking a scalpel blade, I shaved the hair along a line where I would be cutting.

Then, after infiltrating a local anesthetic down a line about fifteen inches long below the spinous processes and behind the ribs, I opened her up.

The northwest wind was probably blowing forty miles per hour and stinging our faces with sleet as the wind blasted the shivering prairie and all its inhabitants.

The calf was coming tail first, so the head and front feet were what I came to first. I got them lifted up, had my client slip on plastic sleeves and scrub up in my bucket of scrub water, then he held onto the front feet while I made an incision in the uterus.

Together, we got the calf's head and front feet through the now foot long hole in the uterus and were pulling it out when we heard the screech of tires on the highway below us.

Someone going by had seen this sight, of two half frozen guys pulling a steaming calf out of a heifer's side and run off the road in their surprise.

I had my client drag the calf around in front of its mother, and she immediately started licking it off.

By the time I got all the layers stitched back together, the calf was licked off, and trying to stand.

We held it steady so it could nurse, then went to pull the bewildered motorist out of the ditch.

Afterwards we eased the heifer and her calf down into a draw out of the wind and left them.

If a calf has been licked off dry and gets some milk in its stomach, it can withstand a tremendous amount of cold.

I drove back to the clinic shivering all the way, with the heater going full blast.

In addition to a multitude of C-Sections that spring, there was the usual number of calves to be pulled, often having to straighten out a head that was back or that had a foot back.

Then there were the prolapses.

Sometimes after a cow had her calf, she wouldn't stop straining and would expel her uterus.

These calls typically went something like this; "Doc, I've got a cow with her calf bed out."

"Is it all out? Maybe just part way?" I would say hopefully.

"Nope, I think it's all out, it's about three feet long." Sighing, I would head out to the ranch, knowing I was in for a lot of hard work that might succeed, and might not.

A full uterine prolapse was a medical emergency, and some of them died before I could get them put back together.

On the other hand, I once saw a cow that had a uterine prolapse which had been out for several days. This was in the summer, and the sun had dried it out until it was like leather.

All I could do was wrap a thin piece of inner tube as tight as possible around the cervix to prevent bleeding and cut the uterus off.

Surprisingly, the cow lived.

Many times, these prolapsed cows were out in a muddy lot and the cow couldn't get up, but at Luther's place it was different.

Luther didn't live that far from the clinic, maybe ten miles, but there was a ridge of rough, choppy Sandhills that could only be traversed by winding around and over seemingly endless miles of sand and soapweeds to get there.

This cow was actually in an old barn, and on clean straw, so that was a treat.

I gave the cow a spinal to stop her straining, got her to her feet and started trying to push back an organ that by now was about three feet long and a foot in diameter through an opening that was only about seven inches.

Although it was cold out, in the barn there was no wind, so I soon worked up a sweat. I had stripped down to my waist before starting and was soon covered with blood and other fluids.

After struggling for nearly an hour, the uterus finally fell back into place. I put some antibiotic pills in and stitched the cow mostly shut, so she couldn't push it back out again.

I could always give more spinal anesthetic, but getting to Luther's place was a challenge, so I didn't want to have to come back.

After cleaning up as best as I could, Luther invited me to come in for coffee, while he paid me.

When we got into the house, I discovered a couple of goats also resided there, and there was a hen roosted on the handle of the coffee pot.

I suddenly remembered that I had an urgent call on the other side of the county, and I wouldn't be able to stay for coffee.

Luther had been a bachelor all his life, and his world was mostly out-doors. A neighbor of his told me once that Luther's sister had visited and was cleaning his house. She wanted to know how on earth she was supposed to clean this bathroom.

Luther told her, "Oh, I'll pull the tractor up with the bucket below the window. You can just shovel everything out the window."

One elderly rancher called me out to fix a prolapse in a cow that was out in a corn stalk field, with no corrals in sight.

When we pulled into the field, he said, "Well, there she is."

I replied, "And what am I supposed to do with her? You'll have to get her in for us to work on her."

"Oh, no problem," the gentleman said, "You rope her, and I'll drive up on the rope and we'll have her."

Although I was skeptical, that's exactly what we did, and it worked out fairly well. The only problem was that by the time I had her stitched back together, her patience was wearing thin, and she rolled me when I pulled the rope off.

The old rancher laughed heartily and said, "That's just her way of thank-ing you, Doc."

Calving season rolled on, and one balmy March night, John L. called me about ten p.m.

He had a heifer that couldn't calve, and he couldn't get her loaded to bring her to the clinic. "Could I come out?"

It was about thirty miles to John's place, so by the time I got there and finished the C-Section, it was nearly midnight.

John invited me in for coffee and cake while he paid me, then he said, "Doc, when you get home tonight, you stay there. There's a bad storm coming."

Now it had been rather nice that night, and even though the wind was picking up a little, I still couldn't imagine a storm on a night like this.

"What makes you think that?" I wanted to know. John took a look at the barometer mounted on his wall. "The barometer is falling fast," he said, "Its sure going to storm bad."

I headed on home wondering about John, but by the time I got to the pavement, twelve miles from his place, the air was full of big wet snowflakes.

Going south about six miles with the wind I could see fairly well although the visibility was significantly decreased.

When I turned west, still twelve miles from town, the snow was blowing so hard across the highway that I had to just inch along from white line to white line.

I finally got home, and the storm was indeed a bad one. It blew for three days, and by the time it was over, the whole country was drifted in.

I heard that west of town there were drifts thirty feet deep. The National Guard had to bring a big boring type snowblower to open up the highway.

The storm knocked out power lines and phone service for a while, and one evening there was a knock on the door.

It was Dick H. He had a heifer that needed a C-Section, and he had somehow managed to drive his little Ford Bronco along ridge tops for several miles to get to town to pick me up.

We drove out to his place which took the rest of the daylight hours and went to his barn where he had the heifer in a box stall.

We got a halter on her, clipped her up, scrubbed her left side, infiltrated a line of local anesthetic through the skin and the muscle layer, but when I got deep enough to hit the peritoneum, the lining of the abdomen, she felt it and kicked me across the stall.

Dick was very apologetic at this rude behavior of his heifer, but I assured him that it was my fault. I knew the peritoneum was very sensitive and should have been on guard.

We got a live calf out, and Dick rubbed it down with straw while I closed the uterus and the muscle and skin layers.

We left the calf with its mother, trying to get unsteadily to its feet and get around to the udder. It was a sight I never tired of seeing, so we stood and watched awhile until it found a teat and began sucking.

As we walked toward the house Dick said, "I'll just check through the other heifers before we go in for coffee."

Sure enough, there was another one calving. We decided to go have coffee and give her a little time, then come back and check.

The storm had weakened all the cattle in the area, so this heifer also needed help, but we were able to pull her calf. Once that calf was up and sucking, we walked through them again, and a third one was going.

In all, before the night was over, five heifers calved; one on its own, two that we pulled and two that required C-Sections.

By this time, the dawn had arrived, and Dick insisted I stay for breakfast, then took me back to town to deal with other emergencies.

SMILING BENNY

B enny ranched out on what I considered to be the edge of my practice area. That area was to expand greatly in a couple of years due to other veterinarians retiring or taking government jobs. More on that later.

Benny ran cows, but also had pigs. He had a number of sows and raised feeder pigs, or sometimes finished the pigs out himself in years when he had a lot of grain.

One of the things I liked most about Benny was his friendly demeanor. He was always smiling. In fact, I can only remember one time when he wasn't smiling.

Benny called me out late one night to attend a sow that was farrowing and had a piglet stuck which he couldn't get out.

When I arrived at his place, he was still smiling, but his smile had a strained look about it. "She's over in the barn," he said, "I tried everything I could think of, but just couldn't budge that piglet."

On entering the barn, I found a huge Yorkshire sow laid out on her side looking like a beached whale, with only two piglets nursing.

After scrubbing both the sow and my arm, I donned a plastic sleeve, soaped everything up good and reached in her.

The problem was soon obvious. There was a piglet stuck cross ways trying to enter the cervix.

The uterus in a pregnant sow is forked at the cervix, and the two horns go left and right from there.

This piglet was stuck cross ways, with another one jammed up tight against it, so I was unable to move it around.

Benny was looking concerned, but still smiling as he watched me work to try and unstick the piglet.

I finally had to admit defeat and said to Benny, "I can't move the piglet. We'll have to do a C-Section."

The smile almost disappeared when I said that.

"Have you ever done one on a sow," Benny wanted to know.

As it happened, I had done one while interning in eastern Nebraska a number of years before, between my junior and senior years of vet school.

"Only one Benny," I replied," but it came out alright."

"Well, go ahead," Benny said, "I'm going to lose her if we don't do something."

The sow was exhausted enough that I didn't really think she would try to get up, but I stationed one of Benny's neighbors at the head to hold onto the uphill front leg, and another man on the uphill back leg. Together, they could hold her down if necessary.

I clipped up an area over the flank, scrubbed it good and infiltrated a line of local anesthetic about eight inches long down her flank.

After scrubbing myself again and donning sleeve and gloves, I made an incision about the length of the local down her side and reached into the abdomen.

At this point, Benny's smile disappeared completely, and he turned very pale. There wasn't time to deal with him at the moment, so I kept going.

I felt along the horn of the uterus until I came to the stuck piglet, then came back toward the tip until just over the second piglet.

I made an incision over the nose of this one, lengthened the incision with blunt scissors, reached in and extracted the piglet, and handed it to Benny.

The smile started to come back on Benny's face.

The stuck piglet was next, and I reached down the uterus to where his nose was and pulled him up to the hole I already had in the uterus, removed him, and handed him to Benny.

This one had gone too long in a position of being pushed against and was not alive.

I stitched up the uterus in that place, moved two piglets down and made a new incision and extracted two piglets, handing them to Benny.

Benny dutifully rubbed each piglet dry with straw and got it up to the sow's udder where it began sucking.

By the time they were all born, we had ten live piglets, plus the one that was dead. Benny's smile got wider and wider with each successive piglet that I handed to him.

After removing all the piglets, I stitched the peritoneum up to within a couple of inches from the top, then poured in a bottle of tetracycline mixed with sterile saline and a little dexamethasone, then finished closing that layer.

This was followed by closing the muscle layer, and finally the skin. I gave the sow a shot of antibiotic to ward off any infection and we were done.

After cleaning everything up, Benny asked me to come in and have coffee while he paid me.

At that time, there were quite a few of the ranchers and farmers who kept pigs, and Benny told the story of his C-Sectioned sow all over the country.

Somehow, he never told how his smile completely disappeared for a while that night, and about how white his face turned until that first piglet came out.

As fate would have it, one of the guys who heard Benny's story had a similar situation a few weeks later.

When I got to his place, I found that his hog barn had slatted floors, and the pit beneath hadn't been cleaned for quite some time. There was no straw, and no smiling owner; just a hired man who didn't seem to care one way or another about the outcome.

The ammonia from the pit below was so strong I could hardly breathe. There was no pleasure in doing that C-Section, so, I just got through it as quickly as possible and left.

It was several days before my lungs returned to normal. I can only imagine what it must have been like for the pigs.

As I said earlier, a couple of years after I came to Martin, the two vets at Gordon, Nebraska, sixty miles to the southwest, retired, and the only one at Kadoka to the north at that time took a Federal job.

This left me in the middle of a big hole. To the west it was one hundred miles to Hot Springs, where there was a veterinary practice.

To the east it was another one hundred miles to Winner where there were two vets.

To the north it was over one hundred miles to my nearest colleague at Faith, and to the south it was well over one hundred miles to the vet at Hyannis, Nebraska.

There were a lot of cows in this vast region, and a lot of ranchers who needed vet work done.

Although I had a Super Cub airplane and could cover a lot of country, there was just too much work for one man to get done, and after a few years of trying, I burned out.

I sold my practice, moved to Spearfish, and started a practice specializing in embryo transfer in cattle.

This took me all over the United States and parts of Canada over the next forty years, until I finally retired from that practice.

BLUNDERS, BLOOPERS
AND MISCALCULATIONS

L et it be known to one and all, that the veterinary profession affords endless possibilities for making one appear foolish. I've had my share.

Roy managed forty thousand cows for Premier Cattle Co. west of the Missouri River in South Dakota. These were on numerous ranches scattered all across the West River country.

Roy himself was a fine man and a good manager, conscientious, hard-working and a man of his word.

Some of the ranches where Premier had cows were not quite so sterling.

Roy had called me a few times that fall to pregnancy test cows, (apparently Premier did not have a staff veterinarian, so Roy used whoever was closest or whoever he could get), so, we knew each other.

On a balmy day in early December Roy called to ask if I could Bangs vaccinate a couple of hundred heifer calves at a ranch up on Red Shirt Table.

We were to start at nine a.m. and since I knew Roy liked to run a tight ship and get things done on time, I figured we would be done by noon, so booked another group to do in the afternoon.

It was a nice day, and forecast to stay that way all day, and since it was a long way to Red Shirt Table, I flew out to the ranch and was there by fifteen minutes till nine.

There were pickups and trailers all over, but no cowboys nor cattle. Roy was apologetic, but there was nothing we could do but wait beside the pole corrals.

We spent a long time discussing what it was like to manage so many cows on so many different ranches, and about the vagaries of veterinary practice.

About ten thirty, a herd of five hundred cows with their calves came thundering over the hill at a full gallop, with around forty yelling riders behind them.

They boiled through the open gate, across the corral, hit the backside of the pole corral and took it out in their stampede, smashing poles and posts alike then disappeared into the Badlands.

Re-gathering them turned out to be hopeless, so Roy put some of the guys to roping heifer calves.

By two p.m. I had vaccinated nine heifers, all on the end of a rope, when Roy finally called a halt to the circus.

Since I was flying the Taylor Craft airplane which did not have an electrical system, I elected to return home, because it would soon be dark, and I had no lights on the plane.

Getting back to the clinic, I called the client that I was supposed to have seen shortly after noon and told him the situation.

I asked if the heifers were still in his corral. He replied, "Yep, they're still here ...., been here all day ....., waiting for the vet."

I apologized profusely and asked him to keep them in and I would be out first thing in the morning.

Talk about feeling like a heel. My miscalculation had cost this man and some of his neighbors most of a day, waiting for me.

Whenever I could, I liked to go to the continuing education meetings offered by the state veterinary association, both to learn new things, and to be able to visit with colleagues. Sometimes one could learn more out in the hall than in the lecture room.

At one equine continuing education meeting there was a professor from another state who described to us his way of euthanizing horses.

Since I occasionally got a call to "put a horse down," my ears perked up. This fellow said that he used two syringes, fifty or sixty cc's, each full of air.

This he injected as rapidly as possible into the jugular vein, and the horse died a smooth and painless death.

Soon after this meeting, a client who lived about forty miles from the clinic called to say he had an old horse about thirty years old that he wanted me to put down.

Aha, an opportunity to try out my newfound knowledge.

I drove out to the place and the client was waiting with his horse by a stack of hay. I injected the two syringes full of air, and just as the professor promised, the horse collapsed.

I listened to the heart and could hear nothing, so assumed success and returned to town. About an hour later I got a call from this client, "Hey Doc, that horse you killed is standing out there eating hay."

It took an extra two hours out of my day to drive back out there and do the job right.

Moral of the story: Be cautious about using new techniques until proven that they always work, especially when I'm forty miles from town.

Following the blizzard in March, ranchers started noticing that the scrotum on their bulls had turned black from the bottom to about halfway up. This was due to the cold wind and snow driving against them from behind.

They assumed that the bulls would be sterile, so began having me test them to see for sure before the bull sale season was over and they wouldn't be able to get new ones.

John called me out to test his, and the young Red Angus bulls tested alright, but the older Hereford bulls, I couldn't get a good semen sample, so assumed they were no good.

The next week, John hauled them to a sale, but had an older colleague retest them before selling.

This Doctor was able to get good samples, and the bulls were fine. John called and told me. He said, "Doc Johnson works his machine a little different than you do."

The next day, I called my colleague, Dr. Johnson and asked if I could go along the next time, he went out to test bulls. He graciously agreed, and I relearned how to test bulls under Dr. Johnson's guidance and further disasters were averted.

SUPERSTITIONS

I thought for a minute that the little man was going to hit me, he was so angry. "It is not those lumps," he fairly screamed, "It's those little green men."

The call had begun early that morning with, "Doc, I've got a good bull that died here in the corral, can you come out right away?"

Now, checking on a dead animal is hardly an emergency, and since I already had two calls ahead of him, I took care of them first.

It was a nice spring morning with a softness in the air and long V's of Canadian Geese winging their way north. Their honking was always a comforting sound to me, and I was enjoying the day as I drove to the ranch where the bull was.

Arriving there, I found the rancher and several of his neighbors congregated around a big dead Hereford bull in the middle of the corral.

There had been a rash of what people were calling "cattle mutilations," recently, and the whole community was jumpy.

"I tell you Doc, them little green men have struck again," the rancher informed me, and the other men nodded solemnly.

"Is the bull insured?" I asked and the rancher assured me that he was.

"Well, before I can sign the insurance form, I'll have to do a full postmortem exam," I told him.

"Well, cut away," he replied, "But I can tell you, it's those Martians again. Your exam won't show anything different."

I sighed. I'd been through this same scenario before in other places around the county and had always been able to find the real cause of death plus explain why the animals had seemed to have been cut on.

Opening the abdomen, I searched through the organs, liver, spleen, kidneys, etc. but found nothing wrong.

Then opening the chest, I found the lungs to be normal and nothing wrong with the major vessels.

When I opened the heart, the problem was obvious. Cauliflower like bumps covered the heart valves, slowing and finally stopping vital blood flow to the cardiac arteries.

It was vegetative valvular endocarditis.

Trying to explain this to the gentleman was futile. "It can't be them little bumps," he shouted, "Look where they've cut on him."

Around the base of the scrotum and around the prepuce the skin had been chewed through by some very tiny and very sharp teeth. I took my scalpel and incised beside the open skin.

"Now, that's what it looks like when the skin has been cut," I explained, "What you're seeing before was where kangaroo mice chewed through the skin after the bull died."

"He died of vegetative valvular endocarditis, and that's what I'll put on the insurance form." I informed him. I doubted that "Killed by Martians" would fly with the insurance company.

One would think the fellow would be happy, as this diagnosis would assure that he would get the insurance payment, but he was not. What he really wanted was the "fame/notoriety" at the coffee shop of having a veterinary diagnosed cattle mutilation, and he was losing his opportunity for fame right in front of his neighbors.

"Why would a mouse chew on him?" the man stuck out his jaw and glared at me.

"They want the salt from sweat that is around the base of the scrotum and from urine that is around the prepuce," I tried to convince him, with as much patience as I could muster.

The good fellow went into a rage. Jumping up and down, he screamed over and over, "It is not done by mice, I tell you, it's them little green men."

It was pointless trying to educate the man, or his neighbors for that matter so I signed the insurance form, "Cause of death, vegetative valvular endocarditis," handed it to him and left with him still yelling, "It was them little green men."

Driving away, the incident reminded me of another similar thing when I was doing my internship between my junior and senior years of vet school.

I had gone to visit the practice one very cold Feb. weekend to see if I would fit with them and they with me.

I was staying with the junior partner in the practice, and we had just finished an excellent supper prepared by his wife, when the clinic phone in his house rang.

It was a local hog farmer, and he was in a panic, "Doc," he yelled into the phone so loud that we could all hear him, "I've got several sows that have died suddenly, can you come out right away?"

We did indeed "come out right away," and were fortunate to not meet any patrol cars, as we would have surely been stopped.

The farmer met us outside as we skidded into his yard and ran ahead of us to the hog barn.

This building was set up with open box stalls that each opened into an alley. At the front of each stall was a short wall that the sows could step over to go outside through a door of hanging strips of rubber, but that was tall enough that the piglets couldn't climb over.

There were several sows, dead in the alley, and two had died as they stepped over the board at the front of their stalls and were half in and half out.

"Doc", the man said, "I think an evil wind came through here tonight and killed my sows, they were alright two hours ago, and now look at them."

It was hard to disagree with him. This was too sudden to be an infectious disease, could it perhaps be some kind of poisoning?

As my prospective boss and I both wracked our brains for some kind of clue, I glanced up at the furnace in the corner of the barn.

Since it was so cold out, the farmer had shut off the ventilation system and had the furnace going full blast.

The exhaust pipe was completely disconnected from the furnace and the carbon monoxide was pouring out into the room. I pointed this out to my colleague.

He went into immediate action. "Open all the doors," he yelled, "Get that furnace shut off, and get the ventilation going."

"My pigs will all freeze if I do that," the farmer declared.

"Well, they will all die of carbon monoxide poisoning if we don't, and we will too, now hurry."

We spent the rest of the evening opening up the barn, helping the farmer carry out dead pigs, and making sure the furnace exhaust pipe was well attached.

I guess in a way it was an "evil wind" that killed the pigs, but "little green men" killing a bull?

Never.

Writing about the incident with the pigs took me back to my internship and another interesting call.

The two partners in the practice both wanted to go to a veterinary meeting in mid-summer and left me to attend to things while they were gone.

I got a call in the early evening from a fellow named Galen who lived not far from the clinic.

He was in his late thirties or early forties and lived with his elderly mother who required considerable care.

Galen didn't leave the house much as his mother couldn't get around and he didn't want to leave her alone.

He said, "Doc, I've got a chinchilla with a broken leg."

I informed him that I was still a student and that both veterinarians were gone for a few days to a meeting.

He said, "Well, I trust them so if they've left you in charge, that's good enough for me, can you come over to the house?"

It didn't take long to get to his house and discover that he had quite a number of chinchillas in his basement.

He raised these for their fur, and the basement was kept really cold to encourage better growth of fur.

The one in question was a blueish gray one, one of his breeding females, and somewhat rare in the chinchilla world, so, more valuable than the rest.

This animal had somehow gotten one hind leg down through a small hole in the bottom of the wire cage and broken both the tibia and fibula, the ends of which were protruding through the skin.

Galen said that in his experience, chinchillas seldom left a splint or cast on, so what were the alternatives?

The lower parts of the leg, below the break were cold, so amputation was the only alternative.

After anesthetizing the little animal, I cleaned up the lower leg, trimmed off dead skin, laid the muscle back and sawed the lower part of the two bones off.

Then after again thoroughly scrubbing the area with surgical soap, I pulled the muscle over the bone stump, sutured it in place then closed the skin.

The little animal made a complete recovery, and Galen told me later that she had a litter of little ones for him.

That was the first and only chinchilla that I worked on in nearly fifty years of practice and I was happy to be able to return her to production for Galen.

PORCUPINE PSYCHOSIS

We live in an area with a lot of porcupines. Most of the time we only see them as a dark colored pin cushion undulating across the prairie, or up in a pine tree chewing off bark and grumbling to themselves.

The problems we see with them is when they tangle with one of our animals. Dogs are the worst as far as getting in trouble. Many times, I would get back to the clinic after a day of working cattle, to be greeted by a dog with a face full of quills.

Cattle are the second most affected, and every year while pregnancy testing cows we would have to stop long enough to pull quills from a cow's nose.

Horses occasionally get hit by quills, and since their noses are so sensitive, I've always sedated them before pulling the quills. Sometimes a horse would not cooperate, even when sedated, and I would have to fully anesthetize them to get the job done.

Cats are either smarter than other animals or are simply more agile, as I've never seen a cat with a face full of quills.

Of my quill removal practice, dogs took up the vast majority my of time. A few would have quills only in their nose and had learned their lesson with one swat, at least temporarily.

Most dogs never learned, and in fact seemed to become psychotic over the incident and got filled with more quills with each encounter.

There is an erroneous belief that since the white part of a quill is hollow, if the end is clipped off, the quill will fall out.

I've seen a lot of dogs that looked like they had a beard of quills that had been trimmed, but none of them ever fell out.

The reason for this is that the distal end of the quill is solid, and covered in barbs that point backwards, so once in the skin, they are stuck and must be pulled out. If left long enough the skin around them will fester and the quill come out, but it takes a long time.

Once, while baling haying, I was baling with a small square baler and noticed there was a coyote following me. As I watched him, he would grab a mouse running out from under the windrow of hay, toss it in the air and seem to swallow it all in one move.

The coyote's nose was full of quills so, I suppose that was the most efficient way of getting food for him.

I was saddling a horse in the darkness early one morning to go help a neighbor. He wanted to start riding at daylight.

In the darkness, as I tried to brush my horse off, he kept shying away from me every time my brush got near his hip and finally resorted to kicking at me.

Throwing my saddle in the pickup, I just went ahead and loaded the horse in the trailer and went on to the neighbor's place.

Arriving there, I discovered that there were porcupine quills in the horse's rump. I don't know if he inadvertently rolled on one, or if a porcupine fell out of a tree onto him.

One evening I got back to the clinic to find a huge wolf-malemute cross dog with a face full of quills in my chute in the large animal room.

This dog was so mean that its owners couldn't handle it and had just hauled it to the clinic in a stock trailer and herded it into the chute.

When I came near the chute, the dog would snarl at me and lunge itself against the side of the chute. There would be no touching this animal until it was unconscious.

I got a rope around its neck and pulled it up tight against the side of the chute, then grabbing a hind leg, I injected general anesthetic into the saphenous vein.

Once it relaxed and slumped to the floor, I gave more anesthetic until there was no more palpebral reflex, so it was deep enough that it wouldn't be waking up while I worked on it.

The animal was too big to lift, and I didn't want to risk him coming to in the exam room, so I just worked on him on the floor there in the chute.

It took quite a while to pull all the quills, and the dog was beginning to stir by the time I finished, so I quickly gave him a big dose of penicillin and dragged him out and into the client's trailer.

I was glad to see that animal leave, and I never saw him again.

The dog that took the prize for numbers of quills over the years was a St. Bernard from up in the Badlands.

He was a big friendly animal, but at least twice a year he would be brought into the clinic with his whole face, chest, front legs and even down his throat full of quills.

There would be so many quills to pull that after getting him down with some barbiturate anesthetic, I would intubate him and put him on gas anesthetic, where I could safely hold him under for hours if necessary.

At times, I had to pull the quills from the back of his tongue before I could get to the epiglottis to intubate him.

It seemed incredible to me that this friendly intelligent animal would become so angry with a porcupine that he would attack again and again. It seemed that he got more each time than he had the time before.

Porcupine Psychosis indeed.

FAINTING CLIENTS
AND VETS

I t has always been interesting to me why people faint in some situations and not in others.

While managing the ranch in Texas, I was going to do a C-Section on a heifer. The boss's son who was about fourteen years old was there and wanted to watch the procedure.

We got the heifer into a squeeze chute which was on a concrete floor in the calving barn.

After clipping an area about twelve inches wide and fifteen inches long on the left flank, I scrubbed her up good with surgical soap.

As he watched, the boy kept up a running chatter of questions and comments about what he was seeing.

Injecting a long line of local anesthetic down the flank, I noticed that the chatter was becoming less frequent and weaker.

When the heifer could no longer feel where I was going to cut, I took a scalpel and laid open the skin about twelve to fourteen inches.

Since I was busy controlling the bleeding and getting through the muscle layer and peritoneum, I wasn't paying attention to the kid.

Hearing a dull thud, I turned around to find the boss's son laying stretched out on the concrete floor, unconscious. Since I didn't have any help with me, there was nothing to do but leave him lay there and go on with the surgery.

It took probably another half hour to get the calf out, stitch up the heifer and clean up enough to go to the kid's aid.

Meantime, he sat up looked around him like he didn't know where he was, then rose and casually sauntered off.

He never did tell his dad about the experience and I didn't either. I'm sure that he didn't tell out of embarrassment and I didn't tell because I wanted to respect his privacy. I figured if he wanted dad to know, he would tell him.

Several years later when I was in general practice, I was doing another C-Section for an older rancher.

The same thing occurred as with the kid, I was just pulling the calf through the incision in the flank when I heard a thump, looked behind me and found the rancher laying stretched out on the clinic floor.

Since he was older, and the calf was out, I stripped off my gloves and sleeves and helped him up when he regained consciousness and into the empty waiting room, where my Mom who ran the office got some coffee in him and he was good to go by the time I finished the C-Section and loaded the heifer and her calf for him.

It wasn't always the sight of a lot of blood that laid the clients out. One evening, a young fellow brought in his dog, a Blue Heeler, with a broken leg.

It was the femur, (the large leg bone that connects to the hip). This can be repaired in two ways; one is called a Thomas Splint which is a kind of crutch that fits under the pelvis with a circle of pipe to keep it in place then runs down under the toe and is taped in position.

These worked alright in dogs that were not very active and in cattle, but in a young active Blue Heeler it wouldn't stand a chance of staying on.

The other method, and the one which I preferred since it couldn't be chewed off, was an intramedullary pin.

The dog was anesthetized, and I intubated him and hooked him up to the gas anesthetic machine to maintain him.

After clipping and scrubbing the area over the break, I opened up the skin and muscle for six or seven inches and began threading the intramedullary pin up the femur.

The pin had a sharp end on it, and I bored it through the top of the bone until I could get my pin driver hooked onto it. Then I lined the ends of the broken bone up and screwed the pin back down and into the distal end of the femur and buried it in the bone.

Meanwhile, the young client seemed to be getting more and more interested.

He was standing right up against the surgery table and leaned farther and farther over my surgical field until he collapsed face first onto his dog.

There was a young man working for me who had helped me in Texas, and he was standing there too. I yelled, "Catch him John," as the client slid down the side of the table.

John dragged him over to the corner and propped him up as I re-scrubbed the surgery site and finished the bone pinning.

There was one large bone chip near the fracture site which I secured to the rest of the bone with a cerclage wire, then closed the incision area, cut off the top of the pin, leaving just enough sticking out that I could get my bone chuck on to remove the pin later, then stitched over the end of the pin protruding from the hip.

The operation was nearly over, with the young client slumbering in the corner, when he shook his head, looked around like, "What am I doing down here," then sheepishly stood up and went into the waiting room.

I knew this fellow's family butchered their own beef and pork, and he was a hunter and had field dressed deer several times.

I guess the fact that it was his pet involved that send him into dream land that day, as I've never known him to be squeamish about the sight of blood.

It isn't only clients who sometimes lose consciousness, vets can also.

I have several allergies and one of them is to Lidocaine. I learned this quite by accident when I was in high school. I needed some dental work done and since the nearest dentist was thirty miles away and I didn't have a car, I hitch hiked there. This was a common practice where I grew up.

Once in the chair, the dentist injected a numbing agent into my gum, then left the room for something.

I started sweating and my heart racing, then the next thing I knew was the dentist slapping me in the face and yelling, "WAKE UP, WAKE UP,"

I had passed out.

The dentist went ahead and finished whatever needed to be done, then asked me if my ride was coming soon.

I informed him that I wouldn't have a ride until I could catch one out on the highway. He was very reluctant to release me, but finally decided that my passing out was most likely due to the Lidocaine he had injected into my gum.

He told me to always tell any dentist I went to that I was allergic to Lidocaine, so this didn't happen again.

For a number of years, I didn't have any more trouble even though I had a fair amount of dental work done. I just told them what I was allergic to and they used a different local anesthetic.

Years later when I was in practice, I was doing a C-Section for a client at the clinic. As I was stitching the skin, the big S curved needle that I used to stitch the skin slipped and it cut my thumb open from the first joint to the tip.

I put on fresh gloves and finished the surgery but could see that this cut needed stitches.

Since it was on my right thumb and I use my right hand to maneuver the needle holder, I wasn't going to be able to stitch it myself.

The client and his brother who was along said they could sew it if I could get some local anesthetic in the thumb and then tell them how to proceed.

Unthinking, I injected the thumb with Lidocaine. As I broke into a sweat, I knew I was in trouble and told them, whatever happens, just get that thumb sewed up.

I came to sometime later and was sitting on a chair with my arm being held down onto the surgery table by the client's brother, while the client was stitching away.

They both had a good laugh at my expense over that incident.

Another time I was putting in embryos on a farm in Wisconsin. There was an old barn that formed one side of the corral. A rock foundation about two feet wide supported the barn, with about a foot of it, making a ledge in the corral, for the full length of the barn.

This ledge was a perfect place to set out my equipment as the squeeze chute was only about ten feet away.

The clinic I was doing the work for supplied all the things I needed including the Lidocaine for giving spinals, syringes and needles.

After giving the first spinal, I stuck the needle cover in my mouth, holding it with my teeth while I got across to the ledge to get the embryo.

I wasn't quite to the ledge yet when I broke out in a sweat and my heart began racing. I quickly sat down on the ground in front of the ledge, but never did go completely out.

It was soon discovered that the needle covers I had all had a hole in the tip, and I had gotten a small amount of Lidocaine on my tongue.

It's funny that this happens, because any of the other "caines" can be used with no problem.

I make sure now to always tell doctors, nurses and anesthetists about my allergy and have not had any more incidents.

At a Sunday afternoon C-Section at the clinic once, I cut the left thumb in the same way as the right one a few years earlier.

I got some Carbocaine injected into the thumb, then asked my daughter to sew it up for me.

She took the needle holder like I showed her, but when she stuck the needle into my thumb, she said she couldn't do it, and ran out of the clinic.

Since my right hand was free, I could do the stitching myself but tying the knots was a challenge.

A SUMMER AT
THE KANSAS XIT RANCH:

I t was in the spring of my sophomore year in vet school at Kansas State University, and I was casting about for some job that would pay decent for the summer.

For the past 3 summers, I had stacked small square bales for the college dairy department through the week and rode bulls at regional rodeos on the weekends, neither of which paid very well.

I got a call one Friday evening from my friend, Ancel Armstrong. Would I be interested in A.I.ing a set of cows in a feedlot at Maple Hill, Kansas for the summer?

Ancel managed the bull stud at Kansas State at that time, and I had worked with him on a couple of smaller A.I. projects before.

I said I would be interested in looking into the project, and Ancel said two of the guys I would be working for were flying into Manhattan the next day.

He would be tied up in meetings all day, so, could I pick them up at the airport and take them to the XIT ranch at Maple Hill?

I said I would.

Now, the Kansas XIT had no affiliation with the famous old XIT in the panhandle of Texas.

That historic old three-million acre ranch that was pay for the builders of the Texas State Capitol building had been sold off twenty years before.

The Kansas XIT was owned by the Adams family, and at that time was managed by Raymond Adams.

I picked up Joe Clark and Frank Crews about noon the next day. They had flown to Manhattan in Joe's V35 Bonanza.

Joe and Frank were the C's of CRC company; the R being Gene Roberts.

Frank was in the insurance business, as well as being a banker at San Antonio, Texas.

Gene Roberts was in manufacturing, mining, and trucking businesses.

Joe owned an implement dealership at Pecos, Texas. He also had irrigated farms in New Mexico, plus interests in a couple of banks.

Joe also liked to buy and sell ranches and cattle. In fact, he and Frank owned a mountain ranch in Colorado that Joe had spent the last six months shaping up to re-sell.

They had a man on that ranch who could A.I., and the original plan was for him to do this A.I. job in Kansas.

This fellow had fallen into dis-favor recently and been fired. It was at that point that Ancel called me.

After picking Joe and Frank up, we had a quick lunch then headed east to the XIT ranch.

We met Raymond Adams at the ranch office, and he drove us around looking at these registered Hereford cows that CRC Company was to buy.

After looking over the cows, we went back to the office to work out details.

The ranch crew was to feed the cows a certain amount of silage mixed with grain in long bunks at the front of the 50 to 60 acre lot they would be in.

They were also to feed a certain number of small square bales of hay each day.

The ranch was to furnish me with a horse and tack and allow me access to the working facilities to A.I. cows or treat any that needed it.

I could keep the nitrogen tank in their scale house along with my A.I. kit.

I was not to interfere with their feeding, which would be done each morning, and they were not to interfere nor help me with my work.

After they had worked out the details, Frank wrote Raymond a check, which he stuck in his shirt pocket, then offered to fix drinks for everyone but me.

Joe had the dubious distinction of resembling Lyndon Johnson. At that time, everyone I knew of considered Johnson to be the worst president the US ever had.

So, with the check in his pocket and a couple of drinks in his belly, Raymond said, "Joe, would you be offended if I told you that you look like Lyndon Johnson?"

Joe gave him a long level look and said, "I'd probably overlook it if you fix us another drink."

I drove Joe and Frank back to Manhattan to their hotel, and over a steak dinner, we worked out my agreement with them.

I was to start the day after classes ended, and work seven days a week until the day before classes began again.

They didn't specify the number of hours per day; that was left to my discretion.

I would keep records of the cows I bred and would get a copy of the records to Ancel at regular intervals.

So, the day after classes ended for that semester, I packed a lunch, and a thermos of coffee, and headed for the XIT about an hour before sunrise.

There was no one at the ranch office when I got there, so I just waited in my pick-up until Raymond showed up.

He took me out and showed me the horse I was to use for the summer, stating that he was six- years old. He had been "broke" to ride when he was two years old, but was kind of "broncy", so no one wanted to ride him. As they had plenty of other good horses, he had been turned out for the past four years.

I couldn't catch him of course in the big pen he was in, so ran him into a smaller one, and roped him.

I got a halter on him, brushed him down good and saddled him, while he stamped his feet and snorted.

I could see the ranch crew, by now assembled, peering out from behind corners, and through doors.

They were waiting to see the college kid get planted into the dirt.

I longed the horse, a red roan, and a well put together animal around me in circles, first to the right, then to the left.

Each time he slowed down, I smacked my rope against my leg, which startled him into bucking a couple of jumps then getting back into a lope.

When he had broken a good sweat, I cheeked him around, and stepped on.

He bucked a couple of half-hearted jumps, then we jogged off down the feed alley, to the immense disappointment of the ranch crew.

For two or three days, no cows came in heat, then one morning, the first one showed heat, shortly after daylight; so, I would need to breed her that evening.

The cows had no ear tags, nor number brands on their hides, but all the cows had numbers burned into their horns.

The numbers were only about one inch tall, so, I had to get close to read them.

At first, I just marked the hot cow in my mind, waited until the feeding was done, then rode along in the feed alley getting numbers, as the cows stuck their heads under the cable to eat. They didn't seem threatened when I was on the other side of the bunk.

As the summer progressed, they became quite tame, and I could ride right up on them to get horn brand numbers.

So, evening came, and time to take the first cow up to the chute to be bred.

I set the gates to get from the feed alley to the chute, and "Roanie" and I went to get her.

As soon as the cow tried to cut back, and I pressured him to get after her, "Roanie" would start to buck.

We tried again, and he did the same thing.

Now, I have always liked horses, and would never abuse one, but that cow had to go to the chute.

So, on the third try, when "Roanie" bogged his head, I drove the spurs into his ribs and over and undered him with my reins.

"Roanie" quickly converted to my way of thinking, and we got the cow out on the next try.

Although he was pig headed in his work ethic, "Roanie" was far from stupid, and he quickly figured out that it was easier to do the job right the first time, rather than having to do it over and over.

Within a couple of weeks, "Roanie" got to be a pretty good cutting horse, and it was a rare cow that got by him.

The hay was fed each morning by a little gnome of a man named George.

George would come clip-clopping down the feed alley driving a team of huge gray mules, that were about as long in the tooth as George was. George was in his eighties.

George had been a fixture on the ranch and did only what he pleased. He would harness the mules in the horse barn and drive them over to the hay barn, where he hitched them to the hay wagon.

When he finished feeding, George would park the wagon in the hay barn and go unharness the mules. Some of the rest of the ranch crew refilled the wagon with bales each day.

The hay racks were out in the center of the lot where the cows were, and George would pull up to the gate and open it, then yell, "Giddup." The mules would walk through but stop a foot or two short of where George could get the gate shut.

George would let go with a string of profanity and yell, "Give a little," whereupon, the mules would take two more steps and stop.

George would then shut the gate, climb back on the wagon, and go feed the bales.

He would drive the wagon up near a hay rack, cut the twine on the first bale, hang the strings over the front of the wagon, then with a pitchfork, put the bale, a few pieces at a time into the rack.

He continued this procedure over and over until all the bales were fed.

Coming out of the lot was the same routine as when they went in. The mules would stop just short of where George could get the gate shut.

He would release a string of profanity and yell, "Give a little," the mules would take two steps and George could shut the gate.

I never, the whole summer saw the mules go all the way through the gate on the first try. They seemed to delight in aggravating George.

One morning, George must have said something that offended them. When they came out into the feed alley, and George yelled, "Give a little," they just kept on going, and went to the hay barn without him.

George really turned the air blue with profanity when that happened.

The lot where the cows were was on the north side of the feed alley. Across the alley were some smaller lots, and in the farthest one east, were a few steers that hadn't fit the load when they shipped the rest.

There was a concrete pit silo just east of this lot, and liquid from the fermenting corn silage ran down into that pen.

There was one steer who would stand for hours, sipping this silage moon shine.

I wondered if when he went to slaughter, they found him to have cirrhosis of the liver from all the alcohol he consumed.

The summer fell into a pattern, leave home an hour before daylight, be in the lot with the cows by daylight, after the ranch crew finished feeding, take any cows to be bred to the chute and A.I. them, then spend the rest of the day riding, looking for problems, and heat detecting.

Part of the deal was the ranch was to furnish creep feed for the calves, but I was to have to put it out.

I would load a couple of the 100pound bags in my pickup, pull in close to the shed where the creep feeder was built, drag the bags in, and string the feed along in the bunks, the calves could get to, but the cows couldn't.

As the summer progressed, and the flies got worse, I took to cleaning the bunks twice a day, so the calves would have fresh, fly free feed.

Summers in eastern Kansas are hot and humid, but along in mid-July, we got a northern front come through, and for two glorious days, the temperature never got over 75 degrees, with little humidity. Then it went back to hot and humid for the rest of the summer.

The summer finally drew to a close, and all the cows had been bred once, with several being twice, and a few even three times.

Classes were to start the next day, so since there were no cows to breed that morning, and none in heat for that night, I unsaddled "Roanie" and turned him out, then went to the ranch office to let Raymond know I was finished with the job.

Raymond said, "I want to say something to you." I thought, "Oh boy, what did I do wrong?"

Raymond said, "You had plenty of chances to cheat those guys this summer, and you never did. I admire that."

I thanked him, shook hands and left, never figuring I would ever see him again.

In late October, Ancel called to say it was time to pregnancy test the cows at the feedlot, would I pick up Joe and Frank at the airport? He would bring Dr. Marion who would do the testing.

Dr. Marion had a national reputation of being one of the best at palpating cows.

When we started, Joe said, "Bill, why don't you put on a sleeve, and follow Dr. Marion; you could learn something today."

Raymond started to protest that this would take too long, but both Joe and Frank were adamant, "Bill is to go into every cow."

Ancel had the records, so he could tell exactly how many days along each cow should be.

Under Dr. Marion's tutelage, I soon picked up on what he was saying, as he taught me about mid uterine artery size, amount of fluid in the uterus, cotyledon size, etc.

About halfway through Dr. Marion said, "Now, Bill, you go in first, and tell me how far along they are."

It took me a few to start getting close, but with Dr. Marion's expert teaching, and Joe and Frank's encouragement, I soon learned.

In fact, I learned more about palpating cows that afternoon, than I learned in a whole semester at school.

I was very grateful to Joe and Frank for giving me that opportunity.

Ancel told me later that he had gotten the few open cows and the calves sold locally, and he sold the bred cows to a guy in Georgia for really good money.

He said CRC Company had done very well on the deal. They must have, because shortly before Christmas, I got a much-appreciated bonus check from Frank.

I didn't hear any more from Joe or Frank for a couple of years, and I was working in a veterinary practice in Nebraska when Joe called one evening.

"Gene Roberts just bought a 10,000 acre-ranch southwest of Ft. Worth, would you be interested in going and managing it?" Joe asked.

I said, "Joe, it sounds interesting, but I still have student loans to pay off; I can't afford a pay cut."

Joe asked what I was making, and I told him. "How about that much plus 50%?" He asked.

Needless to say, I was soon in Texas, where I experienced two years of adventure before moving to S.D.

FROSTY J POCO

I've read that into the life of every cowboy there should come one good dog, one good horse and one good woman.

I've had my one good dog in years past; I still have my one good woman, my wife, Jeanie. My one good horse was Frosty J Poco. We called him Jay for short.

Jay was sired by Poco Cowpoke, by Poco Bueno and out of a Leo mare: solid foundation Quarter Horse genetics.

Jay was a fifteen-hand tall sorrel horse, wide in the chest and heavy in the hind quarters. He could explode out of a roping box and put me on a calf in a few seconds.

Jay was raised by a neighbor of mine while I was in veterinary school. I first saw him in the spring of my junior year.

The neighbor wanted me to try him, and I was impressed, but he was asking three hundred dollars for him as a three-year old, and that was a lot of money for a poverty-stricken student to come up with.

I told the neighbor I couldn't afford the horse at the moment, but if he still had him after I got back from my internship between the junior and senior years, I'd be interested.

All summer, I thought about Jay and visualized how great a horse he could be if well trained for calf roping.

Over the summer, I saved every penny I could, but when I got back to school, the neighbor said he was now priced at four hundred dollars.

Although it was a struggle to scrape up the extra money, by cutting and selling firewood as fast as I could, finally I had the money, and Jay was mine.

Due to the fact that I thought he had so much potential for calf roping, I took him to a trainer that I knew, and he finished Jay for calf roping. This cost me another one hundred dollars, but a lot of my professors wanted firewood, so I was soon able to pay the trainer.

I roped on him the rest of my college days, and though I seldom won much, some of my friends used him also and paid me mount money, so Jay earned his keep.

One classmate in particular, was a really good roper, in fact he went professional for a while after vet school. He dismounted on the right side when he caught a calf, in fact, he just came up out of the saddle and flew past the horse's head, landing running a few feet ahead of the horse. Jay got used to this, and next time I used him and got off on the left, as I usually did, Jay swung his head to the left like he did when Larry dismounted on the right, and nearly knocked me silly.

After graduation, Jay traveled with me to my first job in Nebraska, then on to the second one in Texas.

When I bought the vet clinic in South Dakota, he came along, and when I leased the ranch in Montana, he went there for a few years.

As my kids grew, they all rode Jay, with the girls especially using him in rodeo events.

Besides roping, Jay would run barrels, pole bend and goat tie. The only things I couldn't do with him were steer wrestling and picking up broncs. In steer wrestling, as soon as I started down, he would duck off to the left, as if to say, "If you're leaving me in favor of that steer, I'm gone."

With broncs, he steadfastly refused to get near the flying hooves of a bronc, still bucking. While we were at the ranch in Montana, I was riding Jay and carrying my four-year old son in front of me. My five-year old daughter was on a little bay horse named Butch, and she was riding along with us.

We were far out in the twenty-thousand acre summer pasture one hot August day when a thunderstorm came up.

I could see from the white sheets falling from the clouds that hail was coming. We rode along until I found a depression below a bank about two feet high. There was a big sagebrush bush on the top of the bank, and I knew sagebrush roots went deep into the ground.

I always carried a slicker tied onto my saddle, so got the kids down into the depression, covered them with my body, wrapped the slicker around us all, wrapped the horse's reins around my wrist, and got a good hold on the sagebrush with the other hand.

The storm raged over us, pounding the horses and my back with hail, but soon passed and none of us were any worse for the wear. Although both horses pulled back some, they didn't jerk away, and we were able to ride home.

When we turned back the lease on the Montana place, my cattle were taken to the Slim Buttes of South Dakota for a year or two, then on to Newell to some leased farms there, and finally to a little place I bought at Spearfish, South Dakota. Jay of course went along on all these moves.

At Spearfish, we wintered the cows at our place, but summered them in private meadows high up in the Black Hills.

Jay was now getting well along in years, and during the summers I would take him up to one of the meadows to get away from the heat and flies.

There was a beaver dam in one of them, and whenever I checked on the cows there, Jay was always near the water at the dam; it was his "happy place."

In the early spring of 1995, Jay was now in his late twenties. One day, he came down with colic. Now, he had been prone to colic most of his life, but I'd always been able to bring him out of it by doctoring him and walking him.

This time, nothing I did made any difference, and I knew he had reached the end. I couldn't let him continue to suffer, and though there was still snow on the ground, I wanted to take him to his "happy place" for his final rest.

I stuck a bottle of euthanasia solution, and a syringe and needle in my coat pockets, saddled a big gray horse to break trail, loaded both him and Jay into the trailer and drove up into the hills.

We went until the snow got too deep to drive, then riding the gray and leading Jay, we went on toward the meadow.

When we got near the beaver dam, I tied the gray horse in a willow thicket and with Jay I went on alone.

When we got to the beaver dam, in spite of his pain, Jay looked around as if to say, "Well, finally, I'm home."

There beside the dam, I said goodbye to him, slipped the needle into his jugular vein and administered the euthanasia solution.

Jay gave a deep sigh, sank to the ground and breathed his last.

I sat down in the snow and held that old sorrel head in my lap, stroking his face and noticing how deeply his temples had sunk in with age and how much white hair had come in on his face; and I'll confess, I cried as I thought back over all the places we'd traveled together, all the calves we'd roped and how well and long he had served my family and me.

Finally, when I was nearly frozen, I eased his head off my lap and laid it gently on the ground, then rode away, leaving Jay in his "happy place."

One good dog, one good horse and one good woman. My life has been fulfilled; I've experienced all three.

THE CLASS CLOWN
AND A KISSED MARE

I t was the spring of my senior year in veterinary school, and we were only about two weeks from graduation.

At that point we were going through clinical rotations. I had finished small animal surgery, ambulatory medicine, large animal surgery, etc. and was in my final rotation, equine reproduction.

At that point in time, equine reproduction at Kansas State consisted mostly of trying to get old Thoroughbred mares to have one more colt.

The racehorse owners seemed to operate under the delusion that their next foal would be a Kentucky Derby winner.

They had about the same odds of this happening as they did of flapping their elbows and flying across Kansas, but hope springs eternal in the race-horse owner's breast, so the mares kept coming, and we kept soldiering on.

The problem with Thoroughbred mares is that as they get old, the vulva tips forward, so that what had once been a vertical aperture that dirt slid off of, now became a horizontal aperture that dirt slid into.

This of course set up an infection which migrated forward, through the cervix into the uterus, causing a flaming metritis, so, of course the mare could not maintain a pregnancy.

The treatment for this, and what consumed most of our time in equine reproduction was to wash these mares up, pass a speculum up to the cervix, then carefully introduce what looked like a large Q-Tip through the cervix, into the uterus. This was twirled around several times then carefully withdrawn.

This Q-Tip was streaked back and forth across a blood agar plate until the plate was full, then it was turned 90 degrees and streaked again, so that we ended up with a plate with streaks going east and west, and streaks going north and south.

Finally, we placed antibiotic discs around on the plate and cultured it in an incubator for a few days.

If we got growth on most of the plate, but a clear ring around any of the discs, we knew which antibiotic to treat with.

Then we infused the uterus of the mare, cultured again, infused again, cultured again, over and over until we had killed all the bacteria, or they died of old age, whichever occurred first.

As soon as we got a negative culture, we sent the mare to be bred, then immediately performed a Caslick's operation.

To do this, we put the mare in the stocks, gave her an IV sedative, scrubbed the vulva area up good, and infiltrated a local anesthetic along the lips of the vulva on each side.

Then with very sharp surgical scissors, we trimmed off about 1/8 of an inch of skin from the top to where the vulva became vertical again and stitched the two sides together.

This would heal in about a week, then we would take the stitches out and send the mare home, to hopefully maintain a pregnancy.

There were five of us senior students in this rotation, including a kid named Steve who had been the class clown all through school.

Steve never seemed to take anything seriously and spent most of his time trying to find ways to humorously annoy the professors and his fellow students.

There were many times throughout our school years that the rest of us students would have liked to stuff a sock in his mouth because his antics sometimes got the whole class in trouble.

Equine Reproduction was taught by Dr. Brandt, a man who was small of stature, but large of ego and attitude.

Dr. Brandt considered Thoroughbred mares to be the highest life form on earth, and he considered senior vet students to be the lowest life form.

So, on this day, we had done all the culturing and treating, the mare had been bred and we were ready to do the Caslicks Operation.

The mare was in the stocks, the tail had been wrapped with Vet Wrap and adhesive tape, and woe be unto the student that left even a single tail hair outside the wrap, and the tail tied around out of the way.

Dr. Brandt started the scrubbing process.

Taking a fresh roll of cotton, he tore off large chunks which he dipped in the scrub water and began washing, tossing the used pieces of cotton left and right, behind his back, over his shoulders, and at any student he caught not paying attention.

Nothing like a cold, wet blob of cotton hitting a student in the ear to bring them back to task.

He used most of the roll of cotton, and with his flinging the used blobs this way and that, the clinic floor began to resemble a cotton field ready for harvest. Of course, when we were finished, the students would get the privilege of picking up all this trash.

When he'd wasted most of his roll, he took a fresh one and handed it to the nearest student to continue scrubbing, this continued until four of us had a turn, then Dr. Brandt handed a roll to Steve and said, "Get to it."

Such sincere groaning, such vigorous pumping of his elbows and bobbing of his head.

Finally, Steve said, "Dr. Brandt, how clean do I have to get this thing."

Dr. Brandt roared, "I WANT IT KISSING CLEAN."

Whereupon class clown Steve leaned over and kissed the mare's vulva.

I think that was the only time I ever saw the humorless Dr. Brandt smile. He said, "Well, I guess that's clean enough," and we proceeded to finish the Caslicks operation.

Following graduation, we students scattered to the four winds, some joining practices, some the military and some to academia, and I never saw Steve again, but I also never forgot the class clown and the kissed mare.

OLD UGLY,
ROPING CALVES AND
TYING GOATS

In the spring of 1978, I bought a load of cows from Wyoming to finish filling a pasture that I was leasing.

In this load was a Simmental – Holstein cross cow that was about the ugliest thing I had ever seen. She was gray and white spotted, and had both ears frozen nearly off, plus part of her tail. We named her Old Ugly.

We shortened it to just Ug when talking about her in her presence, so as not to offend her delicate sensibilities.

Since she was about to calve, I kept her in a little pasture next to the vet clinic so I could watch her.

When she calved, she had too much milk for the calf, so I started getting her in each morning, setting a pan of grain in front of her, and milking out enough for the kids needs for that day.

Old Ugly still produced more milk than the kids, plus her own calf needed, so I bought three more calves to put on her. She raised all four calves, plus provided enough milk for my kids.

We numbered the calves one through four, and the kids called them Numero Uno, Deuce, Tris and Quatro. I think they were hearing Spanish on Sesame Street at the time.

While the three purchased calves were somewhat stand offish, Numero Uno was very friendly. The kids could ride him around, and he always came up for them to pet him.

We had a rodeo arena next to the house, and the girls liked to practice breakaway roping, barrel racing and goat tying.

In competition I tied the tail of their ropes onto the saddle horn with a piece of string and tied a ribbon onto the tail of the rope so the flagger could see when it broke away from the saddle horn.

In practice, this meant we would have to catch the calf to get their ropes off, so I reversed the ropes, put the loop around the saddle horn, and using a piece of baling wire made a loop on the tail of the rope. This way, when they caught the calf, the loop would straighten out, and come off the calf, and they were ready to go again.

The girls all liked to goat tie, but daughter Becky Sobolewski especially liked it, and got quite good at it.

She had several practice goats, and one was a young Billy goat.

There was a client who raised goats, but didn't have a male, so I let her borrow the Billy goat, so her goat herd could increase.

When Mr. Billy was returned, his attitude had changed, and he now felt that he was king of all he surveyed. One day he butted one of the girls and knocked her over, which earned him a trip to the barbeque pit.

I had learned from a Mexican fencing crew we hired on the ranch in Texas that goats were really good eating when barbequed.

They would ask me to go to the sale barn every so often and get them a "burriego", their word for goat.

They didn't care what kind, it could even be an old Billy goat, they could still make some really good barbeque from it.

Becky's goats became like pets, but she could still practice tying them.

In the breakaway roping, the three purchased calves would run like roping calves should, but Numero Uno would come out of the roping box, then turn around and come to the girls. So, he got retired from roping practice.

By supplementing the calves with some grain, Old Ugly was able to raise all four calves to weaning age, plus provide enough milk for my kids.

My Mom used to say, "Pretty is as pretty does."

By that standard, Old Ugly was downright beautiful. Any cow that could feed five kids and four calves was "Doing Pretty."

JOE THE PREACHER

J oe is a preacher. Now, mind you, I'm not saying that's necessarily bad; on the other hand, I'm not saying it's necessarily good. I'm just saying he is.

Sort of like a fence post just is a fence post, and a rattlesnake just is a rattlesnake, Joe just is a preacher.

Except for the times I've had to dig holes to set them in, I've always thought fence posts were fairly useful. Rattlesnakes I'm not so sure about. For a while I wondered about Joe.

See, it's the way he laughs. It's like he starts to say Hi, and gets the hic-cups, and goes on and on with both, Hi-iy-iy-iy… all very high pitched, and at incredible volume., and Joe laughs at everything.

He laughed the time he forgot to set the park brake on his old truck, and it rolled down the hill and crashed through the side of his barn.

He laughed when he roped a bull in the pasture, got his thumb caught in the dally, and it popped the end of his thumb off, and his dog ate it.

He laughed when his wife told him she was pregnant for the 7th time in ten years. He just never seemed to stop laughing.

Joe is a big man; tall, and with an immense belly on him.

The first hint you had that Joe was around was the high pitched Hi-iy-iy-iy… in the distance. Then a belly would appear, and after a while, the rest of Joe would come around the corner.

Joe and I were both helping out at a youth rodeo camp near where I lived.

At these camps, kids were taught Bible lessons, and the basics of Christian faith, and were taught the fundamentals of whichever rodeo events they were interested in.

The kids had a boy's tent, and a girl's tent, with at least one, and often two counselors per tent.

They got up early, had breakfast, then some free time, then a Bible lesson, some talking about rodeo, a chapel service, lunch, rodeo all afternoon, free time to clean up, supper, evening chapel service, a snack time and visiting, then to the tents and lights out.

Most of the kids who came to these camps were ranch kids, who were fairly confident in their own skins, and who appreciated a chance to get away from the ranch and play for four days.

At this camp, there was a kid from town who signed up. He was just barely old enough to be there, and insecurity fairly dripped off him.

He was loud and bragging constantly about what he could do.

He was being raised by a single mother; not sure where his dad was, and he was beginning to take the wrong path in life.

He'd already had a couple of brushes with the law, and his mother sent him, hoping he could find some direction at camp.

The "Kid" signed up for saddle bronc riding as his only event.

We had a bucking machine there, where the kids could practice getting in rhythm without the danger of getting hurt while learning.

All the other boys lined up for a turn, and a local bronc rider or bull rider stood by coaching them.

The "Kid" loudly bragged that he didn't need any bucking machine, he knew how to ride broncs. The other boys had just about had enough of him and his bragging, and weren't having anything to do with him, which only aggravated the "Kid's" insecurity.

So, the first day, lunch over, and the rodeo began. When it came time for the saddle bronc riding, the "Kid" drew a big bay horse that was fairly easy to ride but was a bit of a chute fighter.

If the kids sat right down, got their feet in the stirrups, and called for him, he didn't do much more than snort and stamp his feet, but if they didn't get him out fairly quickly, he would start lunging, and rearing up. When that happened, he was hard to get out on.

There were two riders ahead of the "Kid," and when it came his turn, the chute boss told him, "Son, now sit right down, get your feet in the stirrups and call for him."

The "Kid" gingerly sat down, but when the bay snorted, the "Kid" jumped back up out of the saddle.

Again, the chute boss told him, "He's just trying to scare you. Sit right down and call for him, or he's just going to get worse."

The "Kid" started to sit down again, when the bay snorted and lunged forward. The "Kid" again jumped back out of the saddle.

The chute boss was losing patience. "Get in there and call for him", he said. "No, I don't want to," the "Kid" said, and started crying.

At this, all the other boys started laughing. The "Kid" started cursing God and all of us. A big hand shot out and grabbed the "Kid" by the front of his shirt, lifting him off the ground. The "Kid" kicked, flailed his arms and cursed everyone.

Joe set him on the ground and said, "Son, God loves you, and I love you."

The "Kid" took off across the arena toward town, crying, and cussing us all out.

The rodeo went on, and I thought, "Well, that's one we haven't been able to help."

Supper and evening chapel were over, the kids were in their tents and it was about time for Lights Out.

Joe and I were having a cup of coffee before making a final check that all was well around camp, when we saw the "Kid" coming across the arena. He didn't say a word, just walked up to Joe, threw his arms around that immense belly and stood there with his shoulders shaking.

Joe let him cry it out, then in a husky voice said, "You climb up in the sleeper of the semi for tonight Son. I'll have a talk with the boys in the morning."

I don't know what Joe said to the boys, but next day they all tried to befriend the "Kid", showing him how to lift on his rein to stay down in the saddle, how to get in time with the bronc, and squeeze the swells when the horse came over the top of his jump.

That afternoon, the "Kid" drew a different horse. One who bucked harder but was quiet in the chute.

With Joe coaching him, and the other boys cheering him on, the "Kid" sat right down, got his feet in the stirrups and called for the horse.

He only lasted two or three jumps before he hit the ground, but he came up grinning; he had faced his fear and overcome it.

After that, there was a little Hi-iy-iy-iy...., following Joe all over the camp.

When the camp ended, the "Kid" would have to go back into the environment he came out of, but I had a feeling that Joe was going to take the "Kid" under his wing and do some serious mentoring in the years ahead.

I'm still not sure about rattlesnakes, but I've stopped wondering about Joe. To help a kid who was started down the wrong road find his way to the straight and narrow was sure a worthwhile achievement in my book.

No, I don't wonder any more about Joe.

ELLEN'S SONG

Buford Rutherford 4th had a small ranch in the Badlands, far to the north of my vet clinic.

It was a place of austere beauty, especially when the evening sunset played golden rays across the variegated layers of mineral deposits left in the sedimentary soil long ago in the age of the flood of Noah's time.

Buford lived alone in a log house, that everyone said he had built himself. The house was surrounded on all sides by a veranda and was set among cedar trees near the bottom of a long hill.

Buford had about 150 cows, and a small band of foundation quarter horse mares and one stud.

There was also a Redbone hound named Beauregard who lived with him.

Buford was a quiet man, and although he was always ready to help a neighbor, and was at all the neighbor's brandings, he didn't interact a lot with other folks, and always seemed to be carrying a silent pain, though he never complained nor talked about it.

Since Buford was single, and a nice looking fellow, many of the young women of the area would have liked to date him.

But although he was always a polite southern gentleman, he showed no interest in any of them, and they eventually moved on to more promising fields.

Buford raised colts and started them when they were two years old. He would put about twelve rides on them, then turn them out until they were three, at which time he would begin riding them several times a week until he felt they were ready for someone else.

His horses were much in demand with the local cowboys, and some offered to buy them earlier, but Buford steadfastly refused to sell any until they were four years old, and well trained.

Some even offered him more money, but Buford never seemed to be concerned with money, and refused to lower his standards.

We usually gelded the young stud colts in the spring when they were three years old.

One April day, Buford called to ask me to stop by and do the job next time I was in the area.

As it happened, just a few days later I was called out to do a late-night C-section on a heifer, at a ranch north of Buford's.

Since I was close, I decided to go on to Buford's and take a nap in the pickup until morning.

I cut the headlights at the top of the hill, turned off the engine and coasted down in front of Buford's house.

I rolled down a window and breathed deeply of the exotic fragrance of sage and cedar in the moist spring air. I had just stretched out on the seat and prepared to take a nap when I heard the most ethereal sound from the other side of the house.

It seemed to be produced by several violins, with a hint of a cello joining in.

Curious, I slipped quietly from the pickup and walked softly toward the music.

At the southeast corner of his house, Buford stood, playing the violin. He was dressed in a black tuxedo, with black patent leather shoes, and a black top hat.

Beauregard sat on his haunches, gazing at his master. He cast a baleful glance my direction, then returned to watching Buford.

As the arpeggios rose and fell in the early morning mist, the music spoke of an intense and undying love between a man and a woman, but it also spoke of the love that a Creator God has for His fallen creation.

As the final strains echoed down through the canyons and silence ensued, Buford, without looking my way said, "Go on in and get some coffee Doc, I'll be with you in a minute.

A few minutes later, Buford joined me and poured himself some coffee. I said, "Buford, that was the most beautiful music I've ever heard, what was it?"

Buford stared into his cup for a moment, then said, "Let's take our coffee in the library."

As we went through the door, Buford nodded toward a picture on the wall of a stunningly beautiful woman.

She was wearing a lime green dress; golden curls fell down over her bare shoulders, and she had a simple string of pearls around her neck. She held a cello in her left hand.

Beside her picture were three platinum records, which answered why Buford never seemed concerned about money.

Buford nodded toward the picture. "What you heard was Ellen's Song. I wrote it for her just before we were to be married. We were debuting it with the Atlanta Symphony Orchestra.

We had just begun playing when Ellen groaned and fell out of her chair. By the time I could get across the stage to her, she was dead.

This place was our hideaway from the chaos of touring and recording. We hoped to one day raise a family here. Ellen designed the house, and we came here when we could."

I said, "Buford, I'm so sorry, that must be a hard cross to bear, but have you ever considered that you need to take Ellen's Song to the world?"

Buford looked sadly into his cup. "I know Doc," he replied, "today is seven years she has been gone. I play it every anniversary of her death. The

Lord's been dealing with me about it; I think you're right, it's time to go back on tour."

And that's just what Buford did. He hired a young couple, Toby and Lisa to take care of things while he was gone. They had a little boy named Teddy, who began calling Buford "Grandpa", much to Buford's delight.

When fall came, we pregnancy tested early that year and Buford left to go on tour. I followed him as much as possible in Music City News.

Everywhere he played, the critics gave him rave reviews in the papers. Atlanta, London, Paris, Pretoria, all around the world.

When tour season ended in the spring, Buford returned to the ranch. I was there one day to geld the three-year old colts, and we were again having coffee in the library.

Teddy came running in and jumped on Buford's lap. "I've missed you Grandpa," he said, hugging Buford's neck.

The look on Buford's face was one of deep contentment. He had found peace in taking Ellen's Song to the world, and in a little boy who called him Grandpa.

COW CAMP
MEMORIES

In the late 70's and early 80's I leased a 35,000-acre ranch in eastern Montana. The headquarters were near the Powder River. From there a road led to Ekalaka, and a trail branched off and wound through the Red Shed pasture, where a few weathered and rotting boards remained as the only evidence of the shed that the pasture was named for.

The road went on through the long narrow 3,000-acre Sheep Wagon pasture, where only a little of the running gear remained of the sheep wagon where a herder once made his home.

East of the Sheep Wagon pasture the trail went through an old hay field and finally to the "Jones Place" which was a 160-acre horse-pasture and which contained the cabin we lived in during the summers when we were at the ranch.

I spent most of my time there; very little at headquarters. The house at the Jones Place was an old log cabin that had been plastered over and painted. It had a tin roof, covered by several inches of red rock.

The cabin had only two rooms, a combination kitchen/dining room, and a bedroom with two very old and creaky beds.

We soon discovered that we had a resident skunk living under the cabin, which let us know of its presence every time we turned over on those creaky springs.

There was no electricity, so no refrigeration but there was a window box, about two feet by two feet that extended out on the north side. This kept food a little cooler.

There was a wood stove for heating in the cold fall months when we were working cattle there. It also had a propane cook stove, fueled by a 100 lb. bottle that we had to refill from time to time.

Attached to the front of the cabin was a TV antenna. The man who had the lease before me liked to watch a certain "soap opera" on his battery powered TV, which he took with him when he left, but he didn't take the antenna.

There was a windmill just northeast of the cabin where the horses watered, and where we got any water we needed.

To the right of the windmill was a three or four-acre trap where I kept a wrangle horse overnight, to get the other horses in for the day's work. I would then turn that one out and keep a different one in the next night.

To the right of the wrangle horse trap was an outhouse which sat just back from a twenty-foot drop-off. One wanted to be careful where you stepped when going there in the dark.

East of the cabin, the horse pasture opened into the 20,000-acre summer pasture. It was watered by Stump Creek on the north side, a big dam in the middle and Timber Creek on the south.

Timber Creek was boggy, and was narrow in a lot of places, so the first summer we spent a lot of time pulling yearlings out of the bog where they had gotten themselves stuck.

On the southwest corner of the summer pasture the Timber Reserve pasture completed the spring, summer and fall portions of the ranch, and where most of my time was spent.

Once we had sold the calves and pregnancy tested the cows, they were worked closer to the headquarters where all the hay was and where they would spend the winter.

My veterinary practice in South Dakota got busy in the fall, so I left the wintering job to a hired man.

The first summer, I got word from the neighbor to the south that the fence between us was down and we had yearlings getting out.

The next day was forecast to be very hot but I thought we needed to get the yearlings in and fix that fence regardless.

My nephew, Bryan Beachy was working for me that summer, and next morning we had breakfasted before daylight, then while I ran the horses in, Bryan packed us some lunch, and filled our canteens with water.

We saddled up, loaded fencing materials onto a pack horse and headed across the summer pasture toward where I'd been told the fence was down.

The code of the west for fencing is that you stand facing your neighbor at the middle of the fence, then each of you is responsible for the fence to your right. Naturally, the part that was down was to the right of middle, so was my responsibility.

We found where fence was down, got the yearlings back in and started fixing, finding many places that needed attention.

By noon, the temperature was nearing 100 degrees and we still had a long way to go. We ate the lunch Bryan had packed for us, saltine crackers and sardines, drank the last of our water and labored on.

The farther we went, the thirstier we got. By mid-afternoon, I think I would have drunk water from a cow track if I could have found it.

We finished in late afternoon and saw a windmill about a mile away. It was opposite the direction we needed to go, but since we could see the windmill head turning, we loped over to it.

Alas, the pump rod was broken, and though the head turned, no water was being pumped.

Moral of the story; always take extra canteens on hot days and pack something other than sardines and salty crackers for lunch.

It was near sundown when we finally got back to cow camp and could get a drink.

Nephew Bryan had been living at the Jones Place all spring the second year, fencing and getting things ready to move the cows up to the summer pasture.

One day my daughters and I were there, and the girls decided that Bryan's domicile needed cleaning. They gave everything a good scrub, and even washed the coffee percolator out with soap.

While Bryan didn't mind the girls cleaning the cabin, he took exception at having his coffee maker washed with soap. He said it ruined the taste of the coffee. In fact, he let the girls know in no uncertain terms that they were not to touch his coffee maker again.

So, the coffee maker went unwashed for several weeks. Later in the early summer I was there, and we needed to ride in the summer pasture. While I ran the horses in, Bryan fixed breakfast and started the coffee.

Coming back, I found the breakfast made, but no coffee. The water was boiling, but it wouldn't go up through the stem where it could percolate down through the coffee grounds.

We dumped out the hot water and tried to rinse out the stem, but couldn't, so I went to the barn and got a piece of baling wire and reamed out the stem. It made coffee just fine then.

Joe was one of the pack horses we used. He was a big black gelding about sixteen hands tall and stout made. He probably had some work horse blood in him. Since Joe was gentle and easy to catch, I sometimes rode him instead of packing on him.

One evening just after sunset, Joe and I were jogging along a draw, both of us about half asleep, when a deer jumped up from beside a sage brush.

Joe jumped sideways three or four feet and started bucking. I managed to stay on, more out of desperation than skill, and we went on to cow camp, but I thought, "OK wise guy, you want to buck, I'll take you where you can do it right."

The next week was the Rodeo Bible Camp finals in LaGrange, Wyoming, and I hauled Joe down there. My friend, Gary Walker put him in the saddle bronc draw.

As it happened, the kid who was Wyoming High School saddle bronc champion that year drew him. Joe blew that kid out over his head in about three jumps, then continued bucking so hard he was popping the stirrups together over the saddle.

The next day he bucked, but not as hard, and the third day, he quit bucking altogether. He had had enough of rodeo bronc life, so he went back to the ranch to pack horse life. I still rode him occasionally, but never alone. I didn't want to have to walk home.

Barney was a big raw boned Thoroughbred horse that I bought off the racetrack with the idea that the girls could make a barrel racing horse out of him.

This didn't work out, as Barney knew only straight ahead at full speed. It took a lot to get him turned, so I took him to the ranch to earn his keep. He was really rough riding but could cover a lot of country.

Following rodeo season, my friend Gary brought his broncs up to the ranch for me to pasture for a while. In this bunch were some wild ones off the BLM ranges.

Word soon came from the neighbor to the north that one of the wild ones was in his pasture and he hadn't been able to get him out.

Gary came to help, and I took Barney, since he was so fast. We soon located the mustang and tried to work him through a gate to no avail.

We decided our only recourse was to rope him.

This pasture was two full sections, so it was six miles around, and we circled it four times that day.

I was lined out on the bronc and Barney was closing the gap, when the wild one rose up and jumped a washout about eight feet across and nearly the same depth.

We were going too fast to stop or turn, so I raised up and gave Barney his head, and thought, "Lord, I'm coming home."

Barney cleared the washout with inches to spare and we finally got the wild horse roped and through the gate where he belonged.

Barney really earned his oats that day.

WEST TEXAS
QUAIL HUNT

I n the early '70's I was managing a ranch southwest of Ft. Worth, Texas for a fellow named Gene Roberts.

While I was still in vet school, I had worked for a partnership of three guys that included Gene, Joe Clark, and Frank Crews.

Gene had gotten his business start by filling a niche need of putting on flashing for contractors in the post war housing boom in Dallas and Fort Worth.

Over the years, he had parlayed this inauspicious beginning into a major corporation with several interests, including manufacturing, trucking, and limestone quarrying, which is why he had bought the ranch I was on, as it sat on 10,000 acres of lime rock.

One evening, the boss, called to say he was going quail hunting at one of Joe's ranches near Pecos, Texas and would I like to go along?

Immediately I began to envision a day of camaraderie with the boss with whom I didn't get much time since he was so busy.

Then came the kicker, "Oh, and take along whatever you need, Joe wants you to pregnancy test a few cows while we are there."

At 5 am, I met Gene at the corporate office in town, foolishly neglecting to eat breakfast before leaving the ranch.

We hopped into Gene's yellow Cadillac and headed west. Folks who had worked for Gene for some time told me he traded cars each year, always the same style of yellow Cadillac.

I soon began to see why he traded each year. At the rate of speed and disregard for highway conditions with which he drove, it seemed marvelous that a car would last even one year.

Although I had always operated under the notion that Texas was a big state, I soon decided I would have to re-think that belief, as we were covering a lot of distance in a short time.

Of course, the fact that we were going about 120 mph made a lot of difference.

About mid-morning, Gene stopped at a gas station and said, "Let's get some coffee."

I would have liked to add a plate of biscuits and gravy, a steak, and some eggs, but no such luck.

Gene was a small built, thin man who didn't seem to require much to eat, so I guess he didn't consider that I might be hungry.

We got to Joe's place somewhere out in the mesquite desert near Pecos sometime after noon.

The few cows that Joe wanted pregnancy tested turned out to be about 200 cows of the most diverse culture one could imagine.

Most of them were Brahman crosses with horns that pointed every which way, a short fuse, and a vile temper.

They were penned up in a large corral that led to a smaller pen, then to an alley about 30 feet long, 2 to 3 feet wide and about 7 feet high, made from mesquite posts set about every 3 feet with mesquite poles lashed to them with what must have been some of the first barbed wire to have arrived in west Texas.

There was a man on horseback in the big corral who chased several cows into the smaller pen, then pursued them one at a time up into the alley, where I scaled the side of the alley, tested the cow, then climbed back out.

Whoever built the facility must have never considered that one day someone might need to get in behind a cow, so there was no gate into the side of the alley; only one at the end to let cows out.

This climbing over behind each cow was quite cumbersome and I quickly deduced that we would never get done at this rate.

So, I stayed back in the small pen, then when the rider got one in the alley, I would run up the alley, test the cow and leave her in, then run another one in behind her.

When we got the alley full, we could turn the whole bunch out the end and start over.

In theory, the horseman was supposed to protect my back side by staying in the end of the alley, but whenever some old fire breathing "bossy" came at him, he quickly abandoned ship.

Good horses were hard to come by. Vets were expendable as far as he was concerned, so I still had to frequently climb the side of the alley to save my skin.

Finally, about dusk, we finished the job, and Gene came strolling in, whistling, and looking relaxed and happy from his day of hunting.

Tossing my coveralls and dirty boots into the trunk of the yellow Cadillac, I climbed in, scratched, and bruised and still smelling like the south end of a northbound cow, and we roared off, headed east.

I must have dozed off, because when I awoke, I found that we were playing leapfrog with a carload of young guys.

Gene had passed them and had cut back in too soon to please the boys, so they would pass us and cut us off, then Gene would do the same to them.

This was a pleasant enough past-time at 60 or 70 mph, but at 110 it lost a lot of its luster.

Several miles ahead we could see the lights of a town. The boys passed us again then shot on toward the town.

Gene pulled over, got his shotgun and a box of shells out of the trunk, handed them to me and said, "Load this."

This sure wasn't something that I wanted to be an accomplice to, but felt I should, "Ride for the brand," so I loaded the gun, stuck it under the seat, pushed the box of shells as far back under the seat as I could reach, folded up the cloth case and sat on it.

Going through the town, we saw the boy's car, but no boys. A few miles out of town a siren sounded behind us and red lights were flashing.

I began to have visions of spending the night in a West Texas jail, as the law would surely consider me to be an accessory to the fact, if not the fact itself.

Gene pulled over, and the officer cautiously approached the car.

Gene got his driver's license and registration and stepped out of the vehicle. The officer explained that the boys had thought we must be drunk by the way we were driving.

Gene could be persuasive; he didn't get where he was in life by being anybody's patsy.

I couldn't hear what all transpired between him and the officer, so won't comment further on things that were none of my business, but we were soon on the road again, going the speed limit until we crossed a county line, then it was off to the races again.

We got back to town a little before daylight, and Gene pulled into an open café, saying, "Let's get some breakfast before YOU go back to work."

It had been about 36 hours without food, so I filled up good at the boss's expense before he went off to his house for a well-deserved rest and I went back to the ranch to saddle a horse and get to work.

THE SAGA OF
SIMON SLICK

In January of 1973, I arrived in Texas to take over management of a ranch that was owned by a fellow I had worked for one summer in Kansas, while in veterinary school.

The ranch had been owned by a very small, very old Scotsman, who had the whitest hair I had ever seen.

The old Scot had a foreman who ran the ranch for him before it was purchased by my boss. Everyone called the foreman, "Slick".

When he was a kid, Slick really liked a song about a "Rat Tailed Kicking Mule Named Simon Slick." So, his boyhood name had become Simon Slick, which of course everyone shortened to "Slick."

Slick's wife's name was Gladys. She was legally blind and felt her way around with a cane. She also smoked a pipe and dipped snuff. They were quite the couple, and I came to really like them both.

Slick was well past retirement age when I arrived, but he was a tough old cowboy, honest and hard working. I got the OK from the boss to keep him on, and to also give him a raise; so, we were both happy.

The old Scotsman would come out to the ranch from time to time to see how everything was going.

He was driven around in a big white Lincoln Continental, by a very large, very black lady who was constantly smiling.

She tore over hill and vale, rocks and cow trails with utter disregard for the life of the vehicle or its occupants, while the diminutive Scot bobbed up and down in the back seat like a cork in rough water, screeching at the driver, and being totally ignored.

Much of the ranch was covered by mesquite bush, an evil little tree that was coated by thorns about two inches long.

One of our ranch improvements was to get rid of this mesquite. We did this by having a contractor drag about fifty feet of chain that was about as big around as my leg between two D9 caterpillars.

This destroyed everything in its path, then the grass could grow back on the bare ground.

In getting the Scotsman's cows off the ranch, they had missed one big old Brahman – Longhorn cross cow, who would hole up in the mesquite brush, and no one could get her out.

One day the old Scotsman came out and told Slick in no uncertain terms that he wanted that cow accounted for.

By this time, a lot of the mesquite brush had been "chained" down, so there was some open ground.

Slick saddled a little horse he called Shorty and slipped out, catching this old heifer out in the open. I rode along, "just in case."

Slick always wore leather shotgun chaps, leather gloves and a leather coat, summer and winter.

As Slick and Shorty bore down on her, the cow looked up, saw them coming, threw her tail in the air and raced for the nearest mesquite thicket.

Slick roped her just before she hit the thicket. Slick's rope was always tied on hard and fast, and as the cow hit the mesquite thicket, there was the sound of ripping and tearing as the cow, with Slick and Shorty in tow roared through the brush.

I couldn't follow, so went around. They came out the other side into a clearing with Shorty's feet planted and making furrows in the recently torn up ground.

Both Slick and Shorty had been thoroughly combed by the thorns. Slick's coat was shredded, and Shorty had long bleeding furrows along his hips, but both were too mad to care.

Slick finally got the cow slowed down enough to lay a trip and busted the cow onto her side.

I raced in, and while she was still dazed, tied one front leg up tight, then got mounted again before she came after me.

She now hopped on three legs but was considerably slower than with all four feet working.

It took us a couple of hours to work her to the corral, where we could have loaded her. As soon as Slick got his rope off her, the cow promptly tore a hole in the corral fence and took off hopping back toward the mesquite thicket.

Slick went to the house and came back with his rifle. He caught up with her just before she reached the brush and shot her.

"Well, she's accounted for." He said with a grin. This finished the Scotsman's cow gathering.

In the spring, we started artificially inseminating heifers. To do this, we had to catch them as they came into "heat" and take them to the corrals to be A.I.ed.

I was having to be gone quite a bit on cattle buying trips to stock the ranch, so one day asked Slick to "heat detect" for me.

I got back toward evening, just as Slick was riding in. "Did you get me any numbers of heifers to breed in the morning," I asked him.

Slick gave me a strange look, then showed me. All up and down his leather reins, on the backs of both gloves and all over his chaps were complete descriptions of heifers, but not a single ear tag number.

That was the last time I sent Slick to heat detect. I guess there are some jobs that a person is just not cut out for.

As things built up and as we added more ranch improvement projects, we needed more help, and by summer, we had four more guys working.

There was one big young guy who earned Slick's ire because of his aversion to work, and his willingness to stand around and watch others do what he should be doing.

I was going to have to be gone for several days on a trip to California, so gathered the crew up and told them all I was leaving Slick in charge, and whatever he says, goes.

While I was gone, this big kid went to a party on a beach by a local lake. He got too much to drink and started messing around with another man's wife. The husband proceeded to run the kid over with a Volkswagen. (It's a good thing it wasn't a Buick.)

When I got back to the ranch, this kid came to work with his arm in a cast, and his face all banged up.

Slick promptly fired him.

The kid came to me with a sheepish grin and said, "Slick says I'm fired." And looked at me like he expected me to reverse that decision.

I said, "What Slick says, goes." I never saw the fellow again.

I had an Airedale and Australian Shepherd cross dog named "Hustles," who liked to sleep in the back of my pickup. One night, Slick came and got me and said, "There's a heifer calving in the lot by the barn. Looks like she's having trouble."

I pulled the pickup into the lot, with my lights shining on the backside of the heifer. I could just see two feet and the tip of the calf's nose protruding from her. I told Slick, "I'll sneak up and get the calving chains on the calf's feet, then you hand me the calf puller."

All went well, and the heifer stayed down on her side until I began to crank the calf puller.

Then she jumped up, and with the calf puller still attached to the chains began making laps around my pickup.

As she went faster and faster, the flying calf puller banged against the tin barn, and against the pickup. This aroused Hustles, and he jumped out of the back of the pickup just as the heifer came around the corner. She spotted him, snorted and took after him.

So, around and around they went, with Hustles yelping in terror, the heifer bellering' her displeasure with having a dog attend her birthing, and Slick roaring with laughter.

Eventually, the heifer got tired, laid down again, and we were able to pull the calf.

Slick was great help and was still there when I moved to South Dakota.

AIRPLANE ESCAPADES

In May of 1974, I was managing a ranch southwest of Fort Worth, Texas. During that month, I agreed to buy the veterinary clinic at Martin, South Dakota, and move here by August first.

I gave the owner of the ranch two months notice; and he found a new manager in June.

The men working at the ranch kept turning to me for their instructions and ignoring the new manager, even though I encouraged them to switch.

I finally decided to just disappear for a few hours each morning so they would have to work with the new man.

To fill the time, I went to the local airport and took flying lessons. My instructor was a former Navy pilot, and he taught me to fly higher than required, and come in high so that if the engine stalled, I had plenty of altitude to get to where I could land. That teaching probably saved my life a few years later.

The plane we used was a Cessna 150, which is a tricycle gear aircraft.

When I got to Martin, I bought a 1946 Taylor Craft BC12D. It was a "taildragger", that is to say it had a tail wheel instead of a nose wheel like the Cessna had.

This was the first of four planes I would own over the next several years and was the most fun to fly.

It only had a 65-horsepower engine and no flaps. The seat was a piece of plywood bolted to the frame. The doors were held shut by hooks made of number 9 wire.

There was no electrical system, and the gas gauge was a piece of wire that ran from a cork in the tank, up through a hole. I could estimate how much gas I had, by how much wire extended above the tank.

To start the engine, I had to crank the propeller by hand until the engine caught.

One cold morning I was having trouble getting it to start. I cranked and cranked, to no avail.

Finally, in frustration, I gave it more throttle than I should have. That time it caught when I cranked it, but since there was so much throttle, it started rolling away.

As it went by me, I grabbed the strut and dug my heels in. The plane started going in a circle around me, and I was finally able to dive through the open door and back off the throttle.

I stood there shaking for a few minutes before getting in and taking off on a call to some distant ranch.

My instructor in Texas had taught me how to "slip" a plane; to come in high then lose a lot of altitude quickly when necessary.

This is done by "cross controlling", which means turning the yoke left for example, while pushing the right rudder. This made the plane slid through the air sideways, which decreased speed and allowed for a steep descent.

My next plane was a Piper Super Cub. It had a 150-horsepower engine and flaps, so it would power out of really short runways, which were usually pastures or gravel roads.

One day a friend and I flew to a cow sale about seventy miles away. While we were in the sale, a front came through, and the wind started blowing forty to fifty miles per hour.

On the way home, the air was really turbulent, and the plane twisted this way and that, but it didn't take us long to get home, as the wind was at our back.

My friend sitting in the seat behind me got air sick, and since I didn't have a "sick sack" on board, he tied a knot in one sleeve of his denim jacket and used that. I thought that was pretty ingenious, and I appreciated him not getting my plane dirty.

We landed about halfway down the runway and I tried to taxi the rest of the way, but when I gave it a little throttle to roll forward, the plane rose up off the ground.

The owner of the local feed mill, just across the highway who was also a pilot saw what was happening and sent four men over to help me. With two men hanging onto the end of each wing, we got taxied up to the hanger.

That Super Cub would climb like a homesick angel, and one day a different fellow was at the clinic when I got an emergency call to tend a horse on the east end of the county, forty miles away that had cut its leg. We flew out to the place and I got the horse taken care of and we started home.

Not thinking about my passenger, I pulled the plane up sharp at full power since there were trees at the end of the field and climbed steep to about three hundred feet, then leveled off too fast.

The guy behind me was not so ingenious as my earlier friend, and I soon heard and smelled that he was in trouble. We flew on home with the window open.

In the fall of 1978, I sent a bunch of cows to a ranch I had leased in eastern Montana.

Since there was still Brucellosis in South Dakota at that time, the cows had to be bled and tested by a Federal vet in South Dakota before leaving, then be bled again after a certain amount of time in Montana by a Montana licensed vet.

Soon after the cows got there, the weather turned bad with storm after storm and cold.

Time was passing and we were getting near the time when the second test had to be done, so I decided we would have to just "cowboy up", and get the job done regardless of the weather.

There was a guy in Martin who owned a Cessna 172, and since the Super Cub would be too slow for that distance, I rented the 172 from him, and took along a young fellow who had been helping me at the clinic part time.

We landed in Miles City, and someone from the ranch picked us up. It was incredibly cold, but we finally got the job done and got back to the airport. After warming the engine, it eventually started, and we were on our way.

Since it was so cold, I kept my sweatshirt and heavy coat on, and had the heater going full blast.

My flight plan was to go to Belle Fourche, then angle east of Rapid City to Philip, then on home, but before we got to Belle Fourche, fog rolled in and covered the whole Black Hills area.

We skirted along the west side of the hills, looking for an opening, as I really wanted to get home that night.

Over Newcastle, Wyoming I felt myself losing consciousness. As I fell forward, I reached up and pulled open the air vent which was just above and level with my face.

I came to with my young helper slapping me in the face and yelling, "WAKE UP, WAKE UP." I was thoroughly confused and had a severe pain in my chest. My first thought was that I'd had a heart attack and would not make it down alive. Thankfully because of my training by the former Navy pilot, we had been flying about 4500 feet above the ground.

In the time it took for me to come to, we had lost over 2500 feet of altitude. I was so confused that at first, I started to land on the highway, but as my head cleared, I realized that would be impossible on this curving, twisting road.

I remembered from talking to the weather service that it was clear at Gillette, Wyoming, to the west. I turned toward Gillette, started climbing, and started teaching my young friend how to fly, as I really didn't think I would still be alive when we landed.

Gillette has a very long runway, and I called and told them the situation, and that they might have to talk my young friend down, and "Oh by the way this is the first time he has ever been in a plane."

As we went along, with the cold air blowing in my face, my mind cleared more and more and by the time we got to Gillette, I could land fine.

A few days later, the doctor ran EKG's, EEG's and all kinds of other tests, but they all turned out normal. Since I was still convinced that I'd had a heart attack, I sold my Super Cub and quit flying.

Sometime later, my good friend, fellow pilot and client, Dick Howe was at an FAA safety meeting. The instructor there told them, "That young vet that passed out at the controls over Newcastle is a classic example of carbon monoxide poisoning."

My friend Dick did a little checking around and found that the Cessna 172 I had rented had an exhaust leak and the fellow who owned it quietly took it and had the leak repaired but didn't tell anyone. The reason I passed out and my young friend didn't, was that the cabin was closed up tight, the heater was going full blast, and I was very tired and stressed, as it was calving season and I hadn't had a full night's sleep for the past three weeks.

I didn't fly again for a couple of years, but with my friend and fellow pilot's help and encouragement I started back.

Four years later, I turned back the lease on the Montana ranch and moved my cows to the Slim Buttes of South Dakota.

The embryo transfer practice was growing by leaps and bounds, and I often needed to be in one state one day and in another one the next day.

The guy who owned the ranch where my cows now resided had a son who was a pilot and who belonged to a flying club where he could lease planes. I started getting him to fly me to some of these jobs, and as we soon became friends, we decided to partner on a bigger plane, a Cessna 182.

The embryo transfer practice was growing so much that I was using the plane a lot more than he was, so I bought out his share.

The Cessna 182 lasted me until it had too many hours on the engine and would have to be rebuilt or replaced, so I sold it and bought a Cessna 206 from a bank in Sioux Falls, S.D. They had used it for a company plane and were replacing it with a jet.

Over the next several years, the 206 served us well. It would haul six people plus all the equipment and luggage we could stuff into it.

This plane had a turbocharged three hundred horse engine with a variable speed, three blade propellor.

One day after coming home from a trip, I left it sitting at the gas pump to be fueled and check a slight leak on the propellor.

Later that evening, a strong front came through, blowing violently with some rain. I got a call from the airport soon after that my plane had blown over.

Airport personnel had rushed to get all planes inside when they saw the storm coming.

Mine was last, and just as they rounded the corner of the hanger, a gust of wind caught it from the back and blew it over on its top.

My wife and I along with our two-year old son went right out to the airport. Sure enough, there was our plane, upside down.

Our son had a little wooden airplane that he played with nearly every day. From that time on, whenever he got done playing with it, he always parked it upside down.

The insurance company paid me more than I had paid for the plane, and that became the down payment on a place in the country at Spearfish, which in turn became the down payment on the ranch where we are now.

And what of the young man who was with me when I passed out?

A few years later, he married a beautiful young lady in that community. They have raised a fine family and he's part of a successful family corporation, but he still doesn't have much use for flying.

TINY THE MILK COW

When I was eight years old, my Mother had a massive heart attack. The five of us kids still at home were scattered out among aunts and uncles to care for us until she recovered, which took nearly a year.

Sister Martha Templeton gradually gathered us all back up, and finally Mom came home too.

We lived in a "dawdy house"; a house built for grandparents by former occupants, which was attached to the main house by a short, covered walkway.

Sister Martha and her family lived in the main house, and she helped with the cooking and cleaning until Mom gained enough strength to do it.

Not too long after we all got back together, Mom bought a little Jersey cross milk cow, that we named Tiny.

Someone had attempted to dehorn her as a calf, and they got the left horn off, but the right one ended up, a gnarled little stump about 2 inches long.

Tiny used this stub horn to go where she pleased. The only way to keep her somewhere was to convince her that it was her idea to stay.

Mom showed me how to milk Tiny by hand, then turned the chore over to me. I would get Tiny into the barn each morning and evening and milk her, then take the bucket to Mom, who would strain the milk through a dish towel to get out the "floaties", and we had good rich milk to drink.

Mom would skim the cream off the top until we had about a gallon, then we would churn it into butter for use at home.

One evening when I went to get Tiny, I found that she was severely bloated. Cows have four stomachs, with the rumen being the biggest one. That's where the fermentation of grass and feedstuffs takes place. It was sticking high above her backbone.

As things ferment in the rumen, it gives off a gas which the cow belches off periodically throughout the day.

Sometimes, something they have eaten will produce a froth, which does not allow the gas to be belched off. Alfalfa and some clovers can cause this.

When this happens, the rumen swells until it presses on the lungs, and eventually the cow can't breathe, and dies.

There was no veterinarian anywhere near us, but we finally got in contact with a county agent, who suggested I mix a quart of milk with a quart of kerosene and force that down Tiny's throat, then tie a big stick, crossways in her mouth and walk her.

I got a pretty good portion of this concoction down her throat, with the balance getting all over me, tied the stick in her mouth near the back, and started walking her, with her chomping on the stick.

I walked her for what seemed hours, when suddenly I heard a mighty belch, and milk, kerosene, and grass erupted from her mouth.

I think if I could have lit a match in front of her mouth at that moment, she would have looked like the proverbial dragon.

A few more belches, and Tiny was as good as new. I went ahead and milked her, but dumped the milk that night, and the next day, as it smelled like kerosene.

Not too long after this incident, the flooring mill where sister Martha's husband worked laid off a lot of the men, including her husband and Martha and her family moved to Springfield to find work.

About the same time, a little farm came up for sale, just down the hill from where we lived, and Mom bought it. We spent many nights remodeling the old shack of a house and moved there.

Of course, Tiny came with us, and I continued to milk her morning and night. Kid like, I never walked when I could ride, so, when I went to the pasture to get Tiny, I would take a couple of sawmill slats, and hop on her back. I could guide her with the slats and rode all the way back to the barn.

One evening, little sister Becky saw me riding her in, and wanted to ride also.

I said, "OK, when I finish milking, just hang from the rafter above the door and drop onto her back, when she walks under you. Ride as far as the front yard and hop off."

So, Becky hung above the door, and dropped onto Tiny as she exited the barn.

Now, Tiny was used to me hopping on her in the pasture. She was not used to being mounted by an aerial attack.

She went bucking and bellering' out across the barn lot, throwing her head to knock this invader off.

She hit Becky in the nose with her horn, and bucked her off, breaking her arm when she fell.

It seemed that Mom had an uncanny knack for showing up just when some disaster I had caused was happening, and today was no exception.

So, on top of a long hard day of work, now she had to drive sister Becky to Mt. View to the hospital to have her arm set and cast. To say Mom was not pleased with me would be an understatement.

One day, someone dropped off a bushel of apples just before we left for church. Mom set them on the table in the kitchen, and all during church I entertained visions of an apple pie that afternoon, or perhaps some apple crisp.

While we were gone, Tiny, using her stub horn opened the yard gate and came in, to graze in the yard, which still had green grass.

Then, smelling something interesting in the house, she hooked the screen door open and came in.

Finding the bushel of apples on the table, she began to partake.

You've heard the saying, "An apple a day keeps the doctor away, two apples a day brings the doctor to stay."

There's a reason for that statement. Too many apples put the digestive tract into hyperactivity.

What was true in people was also true in Tiny. By the time we got home from church, Tiny had consumed the whole bushel of apples, and was in hyperactivity.

There was recycled apples and grass all over the kitchen floor, the cabinets, the table, and the walls.

So, instead of baking an apple pie, we spent the afternoon shoveling, scraping, sweeping, and washing the house.

Then we did it again, and again, until all we could smell was disinfectant, and not a speck of the mess was left.

As we added assets, Mom bought a Shorthorn milk cow we called Red. This was a wicked beast, who would wait until I was nearly finished with milking her, then step in the bucket, or kick both me and the bucket across the barn.

I found an old set of "Kickers" in the barn and put a stop to her abuse. These consisted of a bracket that fit over the Achilles tendon, just above the hock, one on each side.

There was a chain between them that could be tightened, so if the cow kicked with one foot, it would jerk the other one out from under her.

Red never learned to like me, and I never learned to like her. She was an aggravation all the years that I milked her.

I had saved up money from selling feeder pigs, and when the neighboring dairy sold out, I bought a little Jersey bred heifer. Shortly afterwards, Mom bought one more cow, and I now milked four of them morning and evening.

Mom got a cream separator, and we sold cream that a very large fellow picked up every other day to take to the cheese plant.

So, I milked four cows all the rest of the way through school, but there weren't any of them as interesting as Tiny.

WORKING ON
THE THRESHING CREW

T he spring that I was eleven years old, the creek that ran through our little farm flooded.

This creek exited our place, ran across the road over a low water crossing, along the side of a field, under the railroad trestle, and across the east end of a field that our pastor, who was also a dairy farmer leased and had planted to corn.

The corn was about four or five inches tall at the time, and the water sat on the north end of the field long enough that it drowned out about five acres.

Pastor Oney recruited his son who was a year or so younger than me, and me to replant it by hand.

We each had a shoulder slung sack of seed corn that we could refill at the ends of the rows.

We went along with hoes, dug a small hole, dropped a seed or two into the hole, scraped some soil over it and tamped it down lightly with the back side of our hoe then moved forward eight or ten inches and repeated the process.

It took us about two weeks to finish the task, which time included considerable playing.

There was an old house on this place that our pastor was leasing which was near the corn field. We kids all called it the "haunted house", although the only thing haunting it were rodents, owls and us kids.

There was an orchard near the house that had apple trees and pear trees. In the fall, we all helped ourselves to fruit.

By now, you're probably wondering what all this has to do with working on a threshing crew?

Bear with me gentle reader, we're getting there.

So, when we finished the corn replanting job, Pastor Oney gave me a little runt pig that weighed about ten pounds as my pay.

He must have been fairly satisfied with my work, because when threshing season came around in late summer, he hired me to work on the crew.

I would ride my bicycle to whatever field we were threshing before the dew went off, as starting time was as soon as it was gone.

But before time to pull the threshing machine into a field, the work of cutting and shocking the grain was done.

Someone would go through the field with a "Binder", a machine that was pulled by a tractor or a team of horses, that cut the grain stalks off about four inches above the ground. These stalks went along an "apron" to where they were bound into bundles, probably ten to twelve inches in diameter. These were kicked off the side of the apron as the machine went along.

We boys would take two bundles and stand them on end, leaning against each other, then we would get two more and stand them ninety degrees from the first two, again, leaning against the first ones.

Then we stood four more to fill the holes. So, there would be one bundle each on the north, south, east and west sides, then one filling in the southeast, northeast, southwest and northwest sides.

Finally, we laid two bundles horizontally across the top of our "teepee" of bundles. This was called "shocking" the grain.

We let the shocks of grain dry for several days or weeks until the moisture content was low enough to thresh and store.

Finally, the big day would come. The thresher was pulled into a field by an old F-20 Farmall tractor and positioned where the owner of the field wanted his straw pile to be.

Pastor Oney would unhook the thresher and pull the tractor away, thirty or forty feet, facing the thresher.

He stretched a long belt which was about eight inches wide from the pulley on the tractor to the pulley on the thresher. This powered the machine.

While the bundle wagons were being filled with shocks of grain, he greased up the machine, oiled everywhere that was supposed to be oiled and fired up the tractor.

By the time the first bundle wagon was pulling up to the conveyer that projected from the front of the thresher, the machine was roaring, and the day had begun.

Most places we had both tractor drawn and horse drawn bundle wagons. Sometimes a team of horses were reluctant to get close to the loud machine, and it took two or three tries to get them in place.

Then, one or two of us would be on the bundle wagon, pitching the bundles into the thresher, head end first.

The machine ate the bundles up pretty fast, so we had to hustle right along.

The first year, I was assigned to sacking grain that came out of a spout on the side of the thresher, but soon "graduated" to pitching bundles onto the bundle wagons, or sometimes being on the wagon, arranging the bundles, (shocks) so we could get the most on the wagon.

It was hot, hard work, but I loved it. About mid-morning the farm wife, or perhaps an older daughter would take time from their work to bring a bucket of cookies and jugs of lemonade and tea to the field.

We would take a short break, thank the lady profusely, and get back to work.

At noon, Pastor Oney shut down the thresher and we all went to the house where we were working, to eat dinner.

This usually consisted of fried chicken, that a few hours before had been running around the yard, mashed potatoes with chicken gravy, fresh garden vegetables of tomatoes, cucumbers, green onions, peas or beans and fresh baked bread. There was always several pies or cakes to finish off with.

To a kid who never seemed to get enough to eat, it was heavenly. I would have worked for just the meals and been quite happy, but Pastor Oney paid me fifty cents each evening when we finished.

When the dew began to form, we shut down for the day.

I quickly began to learn the lessons of economics. If I wanted an eight-ounce Coke in a green glass bottle, it would cost me five cents; ten percent of my daily wages.

That was far too much in my opinion, so I saved all my money. By the end of the summer, I had thirty-six fifty cent pieces in a jar in the cupboard.

These, I took over to a neighbor's place who had Yorkshire pigs, and bought a young gilt pig, (a female).

Then, I took my runt pig which was my wages for replanting corn, and which had grown to a pretty good-sized beast by now and traded him for another gilt.

When the two gilts grew up, I trailed them over to the neighbors and got them bred, and soon, I had little piglets running all over.

I was learning the lessons of business and free market enterprise.

I would save one gilt pig to add to my herd, one male pig for butchering for meat for the family and sell the rest.

This money I again saved in a jar in the cupboard, and when our neighbor sold his dairy cows, I went to the sale and bought a registered Jersey bred heifer. When she calved, I added her to the family milk cow herd.

For three glorious years, I was privileged to work on the threshing crew, then combines came into the country, which did all the steps at once, saving a lot of time and work.

I guess that it was progress, but we lost something of community, camaraderie, and wonderful meals in the process.

Today, I see kids coming out of the convenience stores with sixty-four ounce sodas, bags of candy bars, Twinkies and donuts, and I feel sorry for them, knowing that they didn't earn that money they just spent, and they are not learning the lessons of work, saving for the future, and investing what they might earn.

I don't know what the solution is, I'm just glad that I got to experience working on the threshing crew, and the lessons it taught.

AIRPLANE AND
BOAT BUILDING

O f all the hair-brained schemes my brothers and I came up with during our childhood, perhaps the most hair-brained was building an airplane and flying it off the top of the chicken house.

The little farm Mom bought had been sadly neglected for many years before we got it.

There were piles of scrap lumber laying all over, much of it that had nails protruding from it.

There were also piles of old rusty tin that someone had torn off a barn or shed in the past.

These pieces were about twelve feet long, and three feet wide. They seemed to us to be itching to become an airplane wing.

So, we cobbled together a frame which was about ten feet long, two feet wide and a foot high from the junk lumber.

We nailed a board across the bottom for the pilot to sit on, then nailed one of the pieces of tin across the frame, two or three feet back from the front of the frame for the wing.

We were now ready for a test flight.

We hauled the contraption onto the roof of the chicken house and prepared to fly.

It was decided that the lightest one among us should take the test flight, since less weight should equal easier lift.

We recruited little sister, Becky for the first flight. We regaled her with tales of how she would soar serenely out over the yard, "Be sure to wave to us as you go by," and come to rest gently in the pasture.

So, the test pilot was ensconced in the pilot seat, and we gave the plane a mighty push, sliding down the sloping roof toward the edge.

Alas, there were errors in our calculations; instead of sailing gently off the edge, our aircraft plunged nose first to the ground.

Mom came around the corner just in time to see the plunge.

We couldn't tell from little sister's shrieks and screams if she had been merely scratched up or had been cloven in twain.

Since Mom was there, and would know what to do, we thought it might be prudent to observe from afar and were just making our escape when Mom's "GET BACK HERE," stopped us short.

The test pilot was taken in to have her wounds doctored and be consoled with milk and cookies.

We aeronautical engineers were lined up for some continuing education with a hickory switch. No milk and cookies for us.

That brought an end to our airplane building, and we turned our attention to boat building instead.

We would take one of the pieces of tin and bend it over, side to side. Then we would smash the ends flat and bend four of five inches of each end over on itself and flatten it out good.

This should prevent water from entering, right?

Near the middle of our canoe, we would pry it apart and nail a stick about two feet long across, to hold the sides apart enough for us to get in.

We would drag this down to the pond, push it into the water and hop in. With some of our better attempts, we got as much as fifteen minutes of boating before, like the Titanic, our vessel sank to the bottom.

Since the pond was shallow, we simply waded out when our craft sank.

Due to the muddy bottom, and the weight of the water in it, we never got any boats pulled out, and would just build a new one when the urge for boating hit us.

By the time that boating ceased to be interesting, and we turned to other pursuits, there was a whole flotilla of sunken craft at the bottom of the pond.

OF POTATO BUGS
AND CHICKEN THIEVES

When we moved to the little farm Mom bought when I was about ten years old, she hired a guy with a tractor to plow up a big area for a garden.

She would lay out the rows with string, and we would plant vegetables of all kinds there.

In the spring, potatoes began to get "eyes", which is where they would sprout. Each potato might have anywhere from three to eight or nine "eyes."

We would cut the potato up, each piece having an "eye." Mom laid out the row with string, then I came along with a hoe, and made mounds about every foot or so.

In the top of each mound, I planted a piece of potato, with the "eye," up and covered it over with soil.

It was a good year, and in early summer, we had a big, beautiful patch of potato plants growing.

One day, Mom noticed some of the leaves looking ragged. Closer examination revealed potato bugs were eating on our plants.

I don't know if there was a spray to kill them, but we couldn't afford it even if there was, so Mom recruited the "kid battalion," i.e. her children.

She armed each of us with a gallon bucket that had an inch or so of water in the bottom, showed us what potato bugs looked like and told us to pick the bugs off and drop them into the water and to keep at it until we had picked all of them off the plants.

We covered the patch fairly quickly but when we went back to look, the potato bugs had called in reinforcements. There seemed to be just as many as before, so we slowed down, and searched each leaf of each plant.

It was hot sweaty, miserable work, but we soldiered on.

At noon, Mom brought sandwiches, cookies, and lemonade out to the garden, and we took a short noon break.

It was well into the afternoon by the time we captured every single potato bug and were finished with the project.

I took our buckets up to the hen house and dumped them out in the chicken yard. The hens went into a frenzy of feeding on the bugs.

So, the day ended with Mom being pleased, us kids feeling tired, the hens were ecstatic, the potato bugs didn't get a vote.

There was a rather bizarre belief among a small percent – fortunately very small – of the old hard-core hillbillies in the area where I grew up that if I had something, and they wanted it, it was perfectly permissible to steal it from me, as long as they didn't get caught.

Now this was a theology with which I definitely could not concur.

For a week or so, I had the niggling suspicion that I wasn't gathering as many eggs as I should be, but egg laying was a rather nebulous pursuit, so I couldn't be sure. Then one day, a hen was missing.

This could not be tolerated. It was one thing to lose a few eggs, it was something else entirely to lose the factory that produced them. At that time, the line between surviving and not surviving was still too thin. This had to stop.

I started sleeping out in the yard, behind a big tree, where anyone approaching the hen house couldn't see me. I had a shotgun, that I must have borrowed from a buddy. There was only one shell, and I had never fired the gun, but figured it couldn't be that difficult.

After everyone was asleep, I would slip out behind the tree with a blanket, get the shotgun out from under some hay in the barn where I kept it hidden, and wait.

For several nights, nothing happened, then sometime around midnight of the fourth or fifth night, I heard a commotion and squawking from the hen house. I raised up and stuck the gun around the tree, aimed high above the hen house roof – I didn't want to hit anyone, just put a stop to their nefarious activity – and pulled the trigger.

There was a flash of fire, and a mighty BOOM, followed by the sound of someone cursing, and footsteps hurrying away into the night.

It wasn't long before Mom showed up in the yard, wanting to know what the noise was, and why I was out there.

I was trying to explain it to her when she spotted the gun.

"Give me that thing." She demanded, so, I handed it over. Mom didn't have much use for guns in general, and she had none whatsoever for guns wielded by children.

So, I didn't get to shoot anymore. But we also didn't have any more visits from chicken thieves.